D1860600

# BY-WAYS OF BOMBAY

# BY-WAYS OF BOMBAY.

S. M. EDWARDES, C.V.O.

GYAN

*Published by*

Gyan Publishing House
5, Ansari Road
Daryaganj, New Delhi-110002
Phone: 011-47034999, 9811692060
E-mail: books@gyanbooks.com

*Distribution Network*
gyanbooks.com
India, USA, Canada, UK, Australia, France

**© Publisher**

All rights reserved. No part of this work may be reproduced, stored, adapted, or transmitted in any form or by any means, electronic, mechanical, photocopying, micro-filming, recording or otherwise, or translated in any language, without the prior written permission of the copyright owner and the publisher.

ISBN : 978-81-212-9761-5 (PB)
First Published, 1912

2nd Impression 2023

*Printed at:* Gyan Press, Delhi.

The book is sold subject to the condition that it shall not, by way of trade or otherwise, be lent, resold, hired out, or otherwise circulated without the prior publisher's written consent.

**BY-WAYS OF BOMBAY**
Author: S. M. EDWARDES

# BY-WAYS OF BOMBAY.

# BY-WAYS OF BOMBAY.

BY

S. M. EDWARDES, C.V.O.

( *Indian Civil Service.* )

Commissioner of Police, Bombay.

WITH

ILLUSTRATIONS BY

M. V. DHURANDHAR.

( *Head Master, Sir J. J. School of Art, Bombay.* )

1912.

## PREFACE TO THE FIRST EDITION.

The various chapters of this book originally appeared under the *nom-de-plume* of "Etonensis" in the *Times of India*, to the proprietors of which journal I am indebted for permission to publish them in book-form. They cannot claim to be considered critical studies, but are merely a brief record of persons whom I have met and of things that I have seen during several years' service as a Government official in Bombay. In placing them before the public in their present form, I can only hope that they will be found of brief interest by those unacquainted with the inner life of the City of Bombay.

HEAD POLICE OFFICE,
BOMBAY, *June 1912*.

S. M. E.

## PREFACE TO THE SECOND EDITION.

The first edition of "By-ways of Bombay" having been sold out within a month, Messrs Taraporevala Sons and Co. have interested themselves in publishing the present edition which includes several illustrations by Mr. M. V. Dhurandhar and an additional article on the Tilak Riots which appeared in the *Bombay Gazette* in August, 1908. My acknowledgments are due to the Editor for permission to republish this article.

HEAD POLICE OFFICE,
BOMBAY. *November, 1912*.

S. M. EDWARDES.

# CONTENTS.

## ILLUSTRATIONS.

The Spirit of Chandrabai.

I.

# THE SPIRIT OF CHANDRABAI.

## A STUDY IN PROTECTIVE MAGIC.

FEAR reigned in the house of Vishnu the fisherman; for, but a week before, his wife Chandra had died in giving birth to a child who survived his mother but a few hours, and during those seven days all the elders and the wise women of the community came one after another unto Vishnu and, impressing upon him the malignant influence of such untimely deaths, bade him for the sake of himself and his family do all in his power to lay the spirit of his dead wife. So on a certain night early in December Vishnu called all his caste-brethren into the room where Chandra had died, having first arranged there a brass salver containing a ball of flour loosely encased in thread, a miniature cot with the legs fashioned out of the berries of the "bhendi," and several small silver rings and bangles, a coral necklace and a quaint silver chain, which were destined to be hung in due season upon the wooden peg symbolical of his dead wife's spirit in the "devaghar," or gods' room, of his house. And he called thither also Rama the "Gondhali," master of occult ceremonies, Vishram, his disciple, and Krishna the "Bhagat" or medium, who is beloved of the ghosts of the departed and often bears their messages unto the living.

When all are assembled, the women of the community raise the brass salver and head a procession to the seashore, none being left in the dead woman's room save Krishna the medium who sits motionless in the centre thereof; and on the dry shingle the women place the salver and two brass "lotas" filled with milk and water, while the company ranges itself in a semi-circle around Rama the Gondhali, squatting directly in front of the platter. For a moment he sits wrapped in thought, and then commences a weird chant of invocation to the spirit of the dead woman, during which her relations in turn drop a copper coin into the salver. "Chandrabai," he wails "take this thy husband's gift of sorrow;" and as the company echoes his lament, Vishnu rises and drops his coin into the plate. Then her four brothers drop a coin apiece; her sister-in-law, whispering "It is for food" does likewise; also her mother with the words "choli patal" or "'Tis a robe and bodice for thee"; and so on until all the relatives have cast down their offerings,—one promising a fair couch, another an umbrella, a third a pair of shoes, and little Moti, the dead woman's eldest child, "a pair of bangles for my mother,"– until in truth all the small luxuries that the dead woman may require in the life beyond have been granted. Meanwhile the strange invocation proceeds. All the dead ancestors of the family, who are represented by the quaint ghost-pegs in the gods' room of Vishnu's home, are solemnly addressed and besought to receive the dead woman in kindly fashion; and as each copper coin tinkles in the salver, Rama cries, "Receive this, Chandrabai, and hie thee to thy last resting-place."

When the last offering has been made, the women again raise the salver and the party fares back to Vishnu's house, where a rude shrine of Satvai (the Sixth Mother) has been prepared. "For," whispers our guide, "Chandrabai died without worshipping Satvai and her spirit must perforce fulfil those rites." Close to the shrine sits a midwife keeping guard over a new gauze cloth, a sari and a bodice, purchased for the spirit of Chandrabai; and on a plate close at hand are vermilion for her brow, antimony for her eyes, a nose-ring, a comb, bangles and sweetmeats, such as she liked during her life-time. When the shrine is reached, one of the brothers steps forward with a winnowing-fan, the edge of which is plastered with ghi and supports a lighted wick; and as he steps up to the shrine, the relations and friends of the deceased again press forward and place offerings of fruit and flowers in the fan. There he stands, holding the gifts towards the amorphous simulacrum of the primeval Mother, while Rama the hierophant beseeches her to send the spirit of the dead Chandrabai into the winnowing-fan.

And lo! on a sudden the ghostly flame on the lip of the fan dies out! The spirit of Chandrabai has come! Straightway Rama seizes the fan and followed by the rest dashes into the room where Krishna the medium is still sitting. Four or five men commence a wild refrain to the accompaniment of brazen cymbals, and Rama passes the winnowing-fan, containing the dead woman's spirit, over the head of the medium. "Let the spirit appear" shrieks Rama amid the clashing of the cymbals.

"Let the spirit appear" he cries, as he blows a cloud of incense into Krishna's face. The medium quivers like an aspen leaf; the dead woman's brothers crawl forward and lay their foreheads upon his feet; he shakes more violently as the spirit takes firmer hold upon him; and then with a wild shriek he rolls upon the ground and lies, rent with paroxysms, his face stretched upwards to the winnowing-fan. Louder and louder crash the cymbals; louder rises the chant. "Who art thou?" cries Rama. "I am Chandrabai," comes the answer. "Hast thou any wish unfulfilled?" asks the midwife. "Nay, all my wishes have been met," cries the spirit through the lips of the medium, "I am in very truth Chandrabai, who was, but am not now, of this world." As the last words die away the men dash forward, twist Krishna's hair into a knot behind, dress him, as he struggles, in the female attire which the midwife has been guarding, and place in his hand a wooden slab rudely carved into the semblance of a woman and child. "Away, away to the underworld" chant the singers; and at the command Krishna wrenches himself free from the men who are holding him and dashes out with a yell into the night.

Straight as an arrow he heads for the seashore, his hands clutching the air convulsively, his 'sari' streaming in the night-breeze; and behind, like hounds on the trail of the deer, come Rama, the brethren, the sisters, and rest of the community. Over the shingle they stream and down on to the hard wet sand. Some one digs a hole; another produces a black cock; and Rama with a knife cuts its throat over the hole, imploring the spirit's departure, at the very moment that Krishna with a final shriek plunges into the sea. They follow him, carry him out of danger, and lay him, stark and speechless, upon the margin of the waves.

Thence, after a pause and a final prayer, they bear him homeward, as men bear a corpse, nor leave him until he has regained consciousness and his very self. For with that last shrill cry the ghost of Chandrabai fled across the waste waters to meet the pale ancestral dead and dwell with them for evermore : and the house of Vishnu the fisherman was freed from the curse of her vagrant and unpropitiated spirit. "She has never troubled me since that day," says Vishnu ; "but at times when I am out in my fishing-boat and the wind blows softly from the west, I hear her voice calling to me across the waters. And one day, if the gods are kind, I shall sail westward to meet her !"

# II.

# BOMBAY SCENES.

## MORNING.

" Binishin bar sari juyo guzari umr bibin
kin isharat zi jahani guzeran mara bas. "

SO wrote the great poet of Persia:—"Sit thou on the bank of a stream and in the flow of its waters watch the passing of thy life. Than this a vain and fleeting world can grant thee no higher lesson." Of the human tides which roll through the streets of the cities of the world, none are brighter or more varied than that which fills the streets of Bombay. Here are Memon and Khoja women in shirt and trousers (" kurta " and "izzar") of green and gold or pink or yellow. with dark blue sheets used as veils, wandering along with their children dressed in all the hues of the rainbow. Here are sleek Hindus from northern India in soft muslin and neat coloured turbans ; Gujarathis in red head-gear and close-fitting white garments; Cutchi sea-farers, descendants of the pirates of dead centuries, with clear-cut bronzed features that show a lingering strain of Med or Jat, clad in white turbans, tight jackets. and waist cloths girded tightly over trousers that button at the ankle. There, mark you, are many Bombay Mahomedans of

A Millhand.

the lower class with their long white shirts, white trousers and skull-caps of silk or brocade: there too is every type of European from the almost albino Finn to the swarthy Italian,—sailors most of them, accompanied by a few Bombay roughs as land-pilots; petty officers of merchant ships, in black or blue dress, making up a small private cargo of Indian goods with the help of a Native broker; English sailors of the Royal Navy; English soldiers in khaki; Arabs from Syria and the valley of the Euphrates; half-Arab, half-Persian traders from the Gulf, in Arab or old Persian costumes and black turbans with a red border. Here again comes a Persian of the old school with arched embroidered turban of white silk, white "aba" or undercoat reaching to the ankles, open grey "shaya," and soft yellow leather shoes; and he is followed by Persians of the modern school in small stiff black hats, dark coats drawn in at the waist, and English trousers and boots. After them come tall Afghans, their hair well-oiled, in the baggiest of trousers; Makranis dressed like Afghans but distinguished by their sharper nose and more closely-set eyes; Sindis in many-buttoned waistcoats; Negroes from Africa clad in striped waist cloths, creeping slowly through the streets and pausing in wonder at every new sight; Negroes in the Bombay Mahomedan dress and red fez; Chinese with pig-tails: Japanese in the latest European attire; Malays in English jackets and loose turbans; Bukharans in tall sheep skin caps and woollen gabardines, begging their way from Mecca to to their Central Asian homes, singing hymns in honour of the Prophet, or showing plans of the Ka'aba or of the

A Marwari selling Batassa.

shrine of the saint of saints, Maulana Abdul Kadir Gilani, at Baghdad.

The ebb and flow of life remains much the same from day to day. The earliest street sound, before the dawn breaks, is the rattle of the trams, the meat-carts on their way to the markets, the dust-carts and the watering-carts; and then, just as the grey thread of the dawn fringes the horizon, the hymn of the Fakir rings forth, praising the open-handed Ali and imploring the charity of the early-riser who knows full well that a copper bestowed unseen during the morning watch is worth far more than silver bestowed in the sight of men. On a sudden while the penurious widows and broken respectables are yet prosecuting their rounds of begging, the great cry "Allaho Akbar" breaks from the mosques and the Faithful troop forth from their homes to prayer—prayer which is better than sleep. More commonplace sounds now fill the air, the hoarse "Batasaa, Bataasa" of the fat Marwari with the cakes, the "Lo phote, lo phote" (Buy my cocoa-cakes) of a little old Malabari woman, dressed in a red "lungi" and white cotton jacket, and the cry of the "bajri" and "chaval" seller, clad simply in a coarse "dhoti" and second-hand skull-cap, purchased at the nearest rag-shop. And as he passes, bending under the weight of his sacks, you catch the chink of the little empty coffee-cups without handles, which the itinerant Arab is soon to fill for his patrons from the portable coffee-pot in his left hand, or the tremulous "malpurwa jaleibi" of the lean Hindu from Kathiawar who caters for the early breakfast of the millhand. Mark him as

The seller of "Malpurwa jaleibi".

he pauses to oblige a customer; mark his oil-stained shirt, and loose turban, once white but now deep-brown from continual contact with the bottom of his tray of oil-fried sweetmeats: watch him as he worships with clasped hands the first coin that has fallen to his share this morning, calling it his "Boni" or lucky handsel and striking it twice or thrice against the edge of his tray to ward off the fiend of "No Custom." But hark! the children have heard of his arrival; a shrill cry of "Come in, jaleibiwala" forces him to drop the first coin into his empty pocket; and with silent steps he disappears down the dark passage of the neighbouring chal.

Now, as the Faithful wend their way homewards, bands of cheerful millhands hasten past you to the mills, and are followed by files of Koli fisherfolk,—the men unclad and red-hatted, with heavy creels, the women tight-girt and flower-decked, bearing their headloads of shining fish at a trot towards the markets. The houses disgorge a continuous stream of people, bound upon their daily visit to the market, both men and women carrying baskets of palm-leaf matting for their purchases; and a little later the verandahs, "otlas," and the streets are crowded with Arabs, Persians, and north-country Indians, seated in groups to sip their coffee or sherbet and smoke the Persian or Indian pipe. Baluchis and Makranis wander into the ghi and flour shops and purchase sufficient to hand over to the baker, who daily prepares their bread for them; the "panseller" sings the virtue of his wares in front of the cook-shop; the hawkers—the Daudi Bohra of "zari purana" fame, the

A Koli woman.

Kathiawar Memon, the Persian "pashmak-seller" crying "Phul mitai" (flower sweets), start forth upon their daily pilgrimage; while in the centre of the thoroughfare the "reckla," the landau, the victoria and the shigram bear their owners towards the business quarters of the city. "Mera churan mazedar uso khate hain, sirdar," and past you move a couple of drug-sellers, offering a word of morning welcome to their friend the Attar (prefumer) from the Deccan; while above your head the balconies are gradually filling with the mothers and children of the city, playing, working, talking and watching the human panorama unfold before their eyes.

So the morning passes into mid-day, amid a hundred sounds symbolical of the various phases of life in the Western capital,—the shout of the driver, the twang of the cotton-cleaner, the warning call of the anxious mother, the rattle of the showman's drum, the yell of the devotee, the curse of the cartman, the clang of the coppersmith, the chaffering of buyer and seller and the wail of the mourner. And above all the roar of life broods the echo of the call to prayer in honour of Allah, the All-Powerful and All-Pitiful, the Giver of Life and Giver of Death.

## EVENING.

AS the sun sinks low in the west, a stream of worshippers flows through the mosque-gates—rich black-coated Persian merchants, picturesque full-bearded

The "Pan" Seller

Moulvis, smart sepoys from Hindustan. gold-turbaned shrewd-eyed Memon traders, ruddy Jats from Multan, high-cheeked Sidis, heavily dressed Bukharans, Arabs, Afghans and pallid embroiderers from Surat, who grudge the half-hour stolen from the daylight. At the main entrance of the mosques gather groups of men and women with sick children in their arms, waiting until the prayers are over and the worshippers file out; for the prayer-laden breath of the truly devout is powerful to exorcise the demons of disease, and the child over whom the breath of the worshipper has passed has fairer surety of recovery than can be gained from all the nostrums and charms of the Syed and Hakim. Just before and after sunset the streets wear their busiest air. Here are millhands and other labourers returning from their daily labours, merchants faring home from their offices, beggars, hawkers, fruit-sellers and sweet-meat-vendors, while crowds enter the cookshops and sherbet shops, and groups of Arabs and others settle themselves for recreation on the threshold of the coffee-sellers' domain.

There in a quite backwater of traffic a small crowd gathers round a shabbily-dressed Panjabi, who, producing a roll of pink papers and waving them before his audience, describes them as the Prayer-treasure of the Heavenly Throne ("Duai Ganjul Arsh"), Allah's greatest gift to the Prophet. "The Prophet and his children," he continues, "treasured this prayer; for before it fled the evil spirits of possession, disease and difficulty. Nor hath its virtue faded in these later days. In Saharanpur, hark ye, dwelt a woman, rich, prosperous and childless, and unto her I gave this prayer telling her to soak it in water once a month and drink thereafter. And lo! in two months by the favour of Allah she conceived, and my fame was spread abroad among men. The troubles of others also have I lightened with this prayer,—even a woman possessed by a Jinn, under whose face I burned the prayer, so that the evil spirit fled." He asks from two to four annas for the prayer sheet and finds many a purchaser in the crowd; and now and again he rolls the sheet into a thin tube and ties it round the neck of a sick child or round the arm of a sick woman, whom faith in Allah urges into the presence of the peripathetic healer. "Oh, ye lovers of the beauties of the Prophet," he cries, "Faith is the greatest of cures. Have faith and ye have all! Know ye not that Allah bade the Prophet never pray for them that lacked faith nor pray over the graves of those of little faith!"

Hark, through the hum of the crowd, above the rumble of wheels and the jangle of bullock-bells, rises the plaintive chant of the Arab hymn-singers, leading the corpse of a brother to the last "mukam" or resting-place; while but a short distance away,—only a narrow street's length,—the drum and flageolets escort the stalwart young Memon bridegroom unto the house of the bride. Thus is it ever in this city of strange contrasts,—Life and Death in closest juxtaposition, the hymn in honour of the Prophet's birth blending with the elegy to the dead. Bag-pipes are not unknown in the Musalman quarters of Bombay; and not infrequently you may watch a crescent of ten or twelve wild Arab sailors in flowing brown gowns and parti-coloured head-scarves treading a measure to the rythm of the bagpipes blown by a younger member of their crew. The words of the tune are the old words "La illaha illallah." set to an air endeared from centuries past to the desert-roving Bedawin, and long after distance has dulled the tread of the dancing feet the plaintive notes of the refrain reach you upon the night breeze. About midnight the silent streets are filled with the long-drawn cry of the shampooer or barber, who by kneading and patting the muscles induces sleep for the modest sum of 4 annas; and barely has his voice died away than the Muezzin's call to prayer falls on the ear of the sleeper, arouses in his heart thoughts of the past glory of his Faith, and forces him from his couch to wash and bend in prayer before Him "Who fainteth not, Whom neither sleep nor fatigue overtaketh."

During the hot months of the year the closeness of the rooms and the attacks of mosquitoes force many a respectable householder to shoulder his bedding and join the great army of street-sleepers, who crowd the footpaths and open spaces like shrouded corpses. All sorts and conditions of men thus take their night's rest beneath the moon, -Rangaris, Kasais, bakers, beggars, wanderers, and artisans, the householder taking up a small position on the flags near his house, the younger and unmarried men wandering further afield to the nearest open space, but all lying with their head towards the north for fear of the anger of the Kutb or Pole star.

"Kibla muaf karta hai, par Kutb hargiz nahin!"

The Kibla forgives, but the Kutb never!

The sights and sounds vary somewhat at different seasons of the year. During Ramazan, for example, the streets are lined with booths and stalls for the sale of the rice-gruel or "Faludah" which is so grateful a posset to the famishing Faithful, hurrying dinnerless to the nearest mosque. When the evening prayer is over and the first meal has been taken, the coffee-shops are filled with smokers, the verandahs with men playing 'chausar' or drafts, while the air is filled with the cries of iced drink sellers and of beggars longing to break their fast also. Then about 8 p.m., as the hour of the special Ramazan or "Tarawih" prayer draws nigh, the mosque beadle, followed by a body of shrill-voiced boys, makes his round of the streets, crying "Namaz tayar hai, chalo-o," and all the dwellers in the Musalman quarter hie them to the house of prayer.

It is in the comparative quiet of the streets by night that one hears more distinctly the sounds in the houses. Here rises the bright note of the "shadi" or luck songs with which during the livelong night the women of the house dispel the evil influences that gather around a birth, a circumcision or a "bismillah" ceremony. There one catches the passionate outcry of the husband vainly trying to pierce the deaf ear of death. For life in the city has hardened the hearts of the Faithful, and has led them to forget the kindly injunction of the Prophet, still observed in small towns or villages up-country:—"Neither shall the merry songs of birth or of marriage deepen the sorrow of a bereaved brother." The last sound that reaches you as you turn homewards, is the appeal of the "Sawale" or begging Fakir for a hundred rupees to help him on his pilgrimage. All night long he tramps through the darkness, stopping every twenty or thirty paces to deliver his sonorous prayer for help, nor ceases until the Muezzin voices the summons to morning prayer. He is the last person you see, this strange and portionless Darwesh of the Shadows, and long after he has passed from your sight, you hear his monotonous cry: "Hazrat Shah Ali. Kalandar Hazrat Zar Zari zar Baksh, Hazrat Shah Gisu Daroz Khwajah Bande Nawaz Hazrat Lal Shahbaz ke nam sau rupai Hajjul Beit ka kharch dilwao!" He has elevated begging to a fine art, and the Twelve Imams guard him from disappointment.

III.

## SHADOWS OF NIGHT.

THERE are certain clubs in the city where a man may purchase nightly oblivion for the modest sum of two or three annas; and hither come regularly, like homing pigeons at nightfall, the human flotsam and jetsam, which the tide of urban life now tosses into sight for a brief moment and now submerges within her bosom. Halt in that squalid lane which looks out upon the traffic of one of the most crowded thoroughfares and listen, if you will, for some sign of life in the dark, ungarnished house which towers above you. All is hushed in silence; no voice, no cry from within reaches the ear; the chal must be tenanted only by the shadows. Not so! At the far end of a passage, into which the sullage water drips, forming ill-smelling pools, a greasy curtain is suddenly lifted for a minute, disclosing several flickering lights girt about with what in the distance appear to be amorphous blocks of wood or washerman's bundles. Grope your way down the passage, push aside the curtain with your stick —it is far too foul to touch with the hand—and the mystery is made plain. The room with its tightly-closed shutters and smoke-blackened walls is filled with recumbent men, in various stages of *deshabille*, all sunk in the sleep which the bamboo-pipe and the little black pellets of opium ensure. The room is not a large one, for the habitual smoker prefers a small apartment, in which the fumes of the drug hang about easily; and its reeking walls are unadorned save with a chromo plan of the chief buildings at Mecca, a crude portrait of a Hindu goddess, and oleographs of British royalty. It were all the same if these were absent; for the opium-smoker comes not hither to see pictures, save those which the drugged brain fashions, and cares not for distinctions of race, creed or sovereignty. The proprietor of the club may be a Musalman; his patrons may be Hindus, Christians or Chinese; and the dreams which riot across the semi-consciousness of the latter are not concerned as a rule with heroes of either the spiritual or temporal kind.

The smokers lie all over the room in groups of four or five, each of whom is provided with a little wooden head-rest and lies curled up like a tired dog with his face towards the lamp in the centre of the group. In his hand is the bamboo-stemmed pipe, the bowl of which reminds one of the cheap china ink-bottles used in native offices, and close by lies the long thin needle which from time to time he dips in the saucer of opium-juice and holds in the flame until the juice frizzles into a tiny pellet fit for insertion in the bowl of the pipe. The room is heavy with vapour that clutches at the throat, for every cranny and interstice is covered with fragments of old sacking defying the passage of the night air. As you turn towards the door, a fat Mughal rises slowly from the ground and makes obeisance, saying that he is the proprietor. "Your club seems to pay, shet-ji! Is it always as well patronised as it is this evening?" "Aye,

An Opium Club,

always," comes the sleepy answer, "for my opium is good, the daily subscription but small; and there be many whom trouble and sorrow have taught the road to peace. They come hither daily about sundown and dream till day-break, and again set forth upon their day's work. But they return, they always return until Sonapur claims them. They are of all kinds, my customers. There, mark you, is a Sikh embroiderer from Lahore here is a Mahomedan fitter from the railway workshops; this one keeps a tea shop in the Nall Bazaar, that one is a pedlar; and him you see smiling in his sleep, he is a seaman just arrived from a long voyage."

You hazard the question whether any of the customers ever die in this paradise of smoke-begotten dreams; and the answer comes: "Not often; for they that smoke opium are immune from plague and other sudden diseases. But the parrot which you see in the cage overhead was left to me by one who died just where the saheb now stands. He was a merchant of some status and used to travel to Singapore and South Africa before he came here. But once, after a longer journey than usual, he returned to find that his only son had died of the plague and that his wife had forgotten him for another. Therefore he cast aside his business and came hither in quest of forgetfulness. Here he daily smoked until his money was well-nigh spent, and then one night he died quietly, leaving me the parrot." You peer up through the fumes and discern one bright black eye fixed upon you half in anger, half in inquiry. The bird's plumage is soiled and smoke-darkened; but the eye is clear, wickedly clear, suggesting that its owner is the one creature in this languid atmosphere that never sleeps. What stories it could tell, if it could but speak—stories of sorrow, stories of evil, tales of the little kindnesses which the freemasonry of the opium-club teaches men to do unto one another. But, as if it shunned inquiry, it retreats to the back of its perch and drops a film over its eye, just as the smoke-film shutters in the consciousness of those over whom it mounts guard.

Further down the indescribable passage is a similar room, the occupants of which are engaged in a novel game. Two men squat against the wall on either side, surrounded by their adherents, each holding between his knees a long-stemmed pipe built somewhat on the German fashion. Into the bowls they push at intervals a round ball of lighted opium or some other drug, and then after a long pull blow with all the force of their lungs down the stem, so that the lighted ball leaps forth in the direction of the adversary. The game is to make seven points by hitting the adversary as many times, and he who wins receives the exiguous stakes for which they play. "What do you call this game," you ask; and an obvious Sidi in the corner replies:—"This Russian and Japanese war, Sar; Japanese winning!" The game moves very slowly, for both the players and onlookers are in a condition of semi-coma, but the interest which they take in an occasional coup is by no means feigned, and is perhaps natural to people whose daily lives are fraught with little joy. Round the corner lies a third room or club, likewise filled with starved and sleepy humanity. Near the door squats a figure without arms, who can scratch his head with his toes without altering his position. "What do you do for a living, Baba?" you ask; "I beg, saheb. I beg from sunrise until noon, wandering about the streets and past the "pedhis" of the rich merchants, and with luck I obtain six or eight annas. That gives me the one meal I need, for I am a small man; and the balance I spend in the club, where I may smoke and lie at peace. No, I am not a Maratha; I am a Panchkalshi; but I reck nothing of caste now. That belongs to the past."

A light chuckle behind you, as the last words are spoken, brings you sharp round on your heels; and you discern huddled in the semi-darkness of the corner what appears in the miserable light of the cocoanut oil lamp to be a Goanese boy. There are the short gray knickers and the thin white shirt affected by the Native Christian boy; there is the short black hair; but the skin is white, unusually white for a native of Goa, and there is something curious about the face which prompts you to ask the owner who he is and whence he comes. The only reply is a vacant but not unpleasant smile; and the armless wastrel then volunteers the information that the child for she is little more—is not a boy but a girl. Merciful Heaven! How comes she here amid this refuse of humanity? "She is an orphan," says the armless one, "and she is half-mad. Her parents died when she was very young, and her mind became somehow weak. There was none to take charge of her; so we of the opium-club brought her here, and in return for our support she runs errands for us and prepares the room for the nightly conclave. She is a Mahomedan." You

A "Madak-Khana."

look again at the dark-eyed child smiling in the corner and you wonder what horror, what ill-treatment or what grief brought her to this pass. Peradventure it is a mercy that her mind has gone and cannot therefore revolt against the squalor of her surroundings. It is useless to ask her of herself: she can only smile in her scanty boyish garb. It is the saddest sight in this valley of the abyss, where men purchase draughts of nepenthe to fortify themselves against the cares that the day brings. The opium-club kills religion, kills nationality. In this case it has killed sex also!

## IV.

# THE BIRTHPLACE OF SHIVAJI.

ABOUT half a mile westward of the town of Junnar there rises from the plain a colossal hill, the lower portion whereof consists of steep slopes covered with rough grass and a few trees, and the upper part of two nearly perpendicular tiers of scarped rock, surmounted by an undulating and triangular-shaped summit. The upper tier commences at a height of six hundred feet from the level of the plain and, rising another 200 feet, extends dark and repellant round the entire circumference of the hill. Viewed from the outskirts of the town, the upper scarp, which runs straight to a point in the north, bears the strongest similarity to the side of a huge battle-ship, riding over billows long since petrified and grass grown: and the similarity is accentuated by the presence in both scarps of a line of small Buddhist cells, the apertures of which are visible at a considerable distance and appear like the port-holes or gun-ports of the fossilised vessel. Unless one has a predilection for pushing one's way through a perpendicular jungle or crawling over jagged and sunbaked rock, the only way to ascend the hill is from the south-western side, from the upper portion of which still frown the outworks and bastioned walls which once rendered the fortress impregnable. The road from the town of Junnar is in tolerable repair and leads you across a stream, past the ruined mud walls of an old fortified en closure, and past the camping-ground of the Twelve Wells, until you reach a group of trees overshadowing the ruined tombs of a former captain of the fort and other Musulmans. The grave of the Killedar is still in fair condition: but the walls which enclose it are sorely dilapidated, and the wild thorn and prickly pear, creeping unchecked through the interstices, have run riot over the whole enclosure.

At this point one must leave the main road, which runs forward to the crest of the Pirpadi Pass, and after crossing a level stretch of rock, set one's steps upon the pathway which, flanked on one side by the lofty rock-bastions of the hill and on the other by the rolling slopes, leads upwards to the First Gate. At your feet lies the deserted and ruined village of Bhatkala, which once supplied the Musulman garrison with food and other necessaries, and is now but a memory; and above your head the wall and outwork of the Phatak Tower mark the vicinity of the shrine of Shivabai, the family goddess of the founder of the Maratha Empire. The pathway yeilds place to a steep and roughly-paved ascent, girt with dense clumps of prickly pear, extending as far as the first gateway of the fortress. There are in all seven great gateways guarding the approach to the hill-top, of which the first already mentioned, the second or "Parvangicha Darvaja," the fourth or Saint's gate, and the fifth or Shivabai gate are perhaps more interesting than the rest. One wonders why there should be seven gateways, no more and no less. Was it merely an accident or the physical formation of the hill-side which led to the choice of this number ? Or was it perhaps a memory of the mysterious power of the number seven exemplified in both Hebrew and Hindu writtings, which induced the Musulman to build that number of entrances to his hill-citadel ? The coincidence merits passing thought. The second gateway originally bore on either side, at the level of the point of its arch, a mystic tiger, carved on the face of a stone slab, holding in its right forepaw some animal, which the *Gazetteer* declares is an elephant but which more closely resembles a dog. The tiger on the left of the arch alone abides in its place; the other lies on the ground at the threshold of the gate. Local wiseacres believe the tiger to have been the crest of the Killedar who built the gate and to have signified to the public of those lawless days much the same as the famous escutcheon in "Marmion," with its legend, "who laughs at me to Death is dight!"

The Saint's gate, so called from the tomb of a "Pir' hidden in the surrounding growth of prickly pear, is the largest of all the gates and is formed of splendid slabs of dressed stone, each about 8 feet in length. On either side of the gateway are rectangular recesses, which were doubtless used as dwellings or guard-rooms by the soldiers in charge of the gate. Thence the pathway divides; one track, intended for cavalry, leading round to the north-western side of the hill, and the other for foot-passengers, composed of rock-hewn steps and passing directly upwards to the Shivabai gate, where still hangs the great teak-door, studded with iron spikes, against which the mad elephants of an opposing force might fruitlessly hurl their titanic bulk.

Leaving for a moment the direct path, which climbs to the crest of the hill past the Buddhist caves and cisterns, we walk along a dainty terrace lined with champak and sandalwood trees and passing under a carved stone gateway halt before the shrine dedicated to Shivaji's family goddess. The dark inner shrine must have once been a Buddhist cave, carved out of the wall of rock ; and to it later generations added the outer hall, with its carved pillars of teakwood, which hangs over the very edge of a precipitous descent. Repairs to the shrine are at present in progress; and on the day of our visit two bullocks were tethered in the outer chamber, the materials of the stone-mason were lying here and there among the carved pillars, and a painfully modern stone wall is rising in face of the austere threshold of the inner sanctuary. The lintel of the shrine is surmounted wtth inferior coloured pictures of Hindu deities, and two printed and tolerably faithful portraits of the great Maratha chieftain.

"Thence," in the words of the poet, "we turned and slowly clomb the last hard footstep of that iron crag," and traversing the seventh and last gate reached the ruined *Ambarkhana* or Elephant-stable on the hill top. It is a picture of great desolation which meets the eye. The fragment of a wall or plinth, covered with rank creepers, an archway of which the stones are sagging into final disruption, and many a tumulus of coarse brown grass are all that remain of the wide buildings which once surrounded the *Ambarkhana.* The latter, gray and time-scarred, still rears on high its double row of arched vaults; but Vandalism, in the guise of the local shepherd and grass-cutter, has claimed it as her own and has bricked up in the rudest fashion, for the shelter of goats and kine, the pointed stone arches which were once its pride.

Another noteworthy feature of the summit of the hill is a collection of stone cisterns of varying ages, still containing water. The smaller open cisterns, in whjch the water is thick and covered with slime, are of Musalman origin, but there are one or two in other parts of the hill which clearly date from Buddhist ages and are coeval with the rock-cells. The most important and interesting of all are four large reservoirs, supported on massive pillars and hewn out of the side of the hill, which date from about 1100 A.D., and were in all probability built by the Yadav dynasty of Deogiri. One of them known as Ganga and Jamna is full of clear cool water which, the people say, is excellent for drinking. Here again the hand of the andal has not been idle; for such names as Gopal, Ramchandra, etc., are scrawled in English characters over the face of the chief reservoir- the holiday work no doubt of school-boys from Junnar. The presence of these four reservoirs, coupled with other disappearing clues, proves that between the Buddhist era and the date of the Musulman conquest, the hill must have been fortifiedand held by Hindu chieftains, probably the Yadavas already mentioned. The purely

Musulman remains include the *Ambarkhana*, a prayer-wall or *Idga*, the skeleton of a mosque, with a delicate flying arch, and a domed tomb. In front of the prayer wall still stands the stone pulpit from which the *moulvis* of the fortress preached and intoned the daily prayers; but neither the prayer-wall nor the mosque have withstood the attacks of time as bravely as the tomb. For here scarce a stone has become displaced, and the four pointed arches which rise upwards to the circular dome are as unblemished as on the day when the builder gazed upon his finished work and found it good. The *Gazetteer* speaks of it as a man's tomb; but the flat burial-slab within the arches points to it being a woman's grave; and local tradition declares that it is the body of the mother of one Daulat Khan which lies here. Had those she left behind sought to bring peace to her dust, they could have chosen no more fitting site for her entombment. For each face of the grave commands a wide prospect of mountain and valley, the massive hills rising tier after tier in the distance until they are but faint shadows on the horizon; the intense solitude peculiar to mountain-country is broken but fitfully by the wild-dove's lamentation; and even when the sun in mid-heaven beats down fiercely upon the grassy barrows of the hill top, the breeze blows chill through the open arches and the dome casts a deep shadow over all.

At a little distance from the flying-arch mosque are two rooms built of stone, in one of which according to our Muhammadan guide Shivaji was born. Whether it was actually upon the rough walls of this small chamber that Shivaji's eyes first rested is open to considerable doubt, and probably they are but a small portion of a once spacious mansion which covered the surrounding area, now relic-strewn and desolate, and in which the family of the chieftain resided. These crumbling halls, the shrine of Shivabai, and the outwork at the extreme north point of the hill are the only remains directly connected with Maratha supremacy. The outwork which overhangs the sheer northern scarp performed the same function as the famous Tarpeian Rock of old Rome. Thence the malefactor of Maratha days was hurled down to swift death; and history records one instance of seven outlaws being cast "unrespited, unpitied, unreprieved" into space from this inaccessible eyrie by an officer of the Peshwa. Viewed from this point the whole plain seems a vast brown sea streaked here and there with green; and the smaller hills rise like islands from it, their feet folded in the mist which creeps across the levels. To the north beyond the larger ranges which encircle the valley the peak of Harischandragad is dimly visible, towering above the Sahyadris; and across the plain to eastward the Suleman range ends in the huge rounded shoulders of the Ganesh Lena spur.

Shivner has known many changes. It gave shelter to the Buddhist in the first and second centuries of the Christian era; It was excavated and fortified by early Hindu Kings who in turn yielded place to the "imperial banditti," and they held it until the English came and cried a truce to the old fierce wars. And all these have left traces of their sovereignty amid the rocks, the grass and the rank weeds of the hill. It is a living illustration of the words of the poet :—

> " Think, in this batter'd Caravanserai
> Whose Portals are alternate Night and Day,
> How Sultan after Sultan with his Pomp,
> Abode his destined Hour and went his way."

V.

# THE STORY OF IMTIAZAN.

THE scene of her earliest memories was a small room with spotless floor-cloth, the windows whereof looked out upon the foliage of "ber" and tamarind. During the day a black-bearded man would recline upon the cushions, idly fondling her and calling her "Piyari" (dearest); and at night a pretty young woman would place her in a brightly-painted "jhula" (swinging-cot) and sing her to sleep. Then the scene changes. He of the black beard is away, and the form of the beloved lies stark beneath a white sheet while mysterious women folk go to and fro within the house. A kindly-faced old man, who in earlier days had helped her build little dust-heaps beneath the trees, takes her from the warm cot and hands her over to a woman of stern face and rasping tongue, with whom she dwells disconsolate until one fateful day she finds herself alone in a market-place, weeping the passionate tears of the waif and orphan. But deliverance is at hand. The sight of the weeping child touches a chord in the heart of Gowhar Jan, the famous dancing girl of Lahore. She takes the orphan home, christens her Imtiazan, and does her best to blunt the evil memories of her desertion.

Gowhar Jan did her duty by the child according

to her lights. She engaged the best "Gawayyas" to teach her music, the best "Kath-thaks" to teach her dancing, the best "Ustads" to teach her elocution and deportment, and the best of Munshis to ground her in Urdu and Persian *belles lettres*; so that when Imtiazan reached her fifteenth year her accomplishments were noised abroad in the bazaar. Beautiful too she was, with the fair complexion of the border-races, slightly aquiline nose, large dark eyes and raven hair, the latter unadorned and drawn simply back in accordance with the custom of her mother's people which forbids the unmarried girl to part her hair or deck it with flowers. Her Indo-Punjabi dress,—the loose many-folded trousers, the white bodice and the silver-bordered scarf of rose pink—but added to her charm. Yet was Gowhar Jan troubled at heart, for the girl was in her eyes too modest, too retiring, and cared not at all whether her songs and dances found favour with the rich landholders, Sikh Sardars and the sons of Babu millionaires, who crowded to Gowhar Jan's house. "Alas," sighed Gowhar Jan, "she will never be like Chanda Malika, gay, witty and famous for generations; her education has been wasted, and her name will die!" But Imtiazan only pouted and answered; "I care not to throw good saffron before asses!"

Then Fate cast the die. Her Munshi one day brought to the house a Musulman, dressed in the modern attire of young India, who had acquired such skill in playing the "Sitar", that he was able straightway and without mistake to accompany Imtiazan's most

Imtiazan.

difficult songs. Thereafter he came often to the house and gradually played himself into the affection of the young girl, who after some hesitation consented to marry him and elope with him to a distant city. Thus Imtiazan left the house of her girlhood and fled with her husband to Bombay. Money they had not, wherefore Imtiazan, not without a pang, sold her necklace of gold beads and bravely started house-keeping in the one small room they chose as their home, while he went forth to seek employment worthy of his degree at the Calcutta University and of his Rohilla ancestry But alas! work came not to his hands: and as the money slowly dwindled, he grew morose and irritable and often made her weep silently as she sat stitching the embroidery designed to provide the daily meal. She knew full well that vain pride baulked his employment; and after many a struggle she prevailed upon him to become a letter-writer. "An under-graduate, who has read Herbert Spencer, Comte and Voltaire," said he, "cannot demean himself to letter-writing for the public," to which she justly replied that an education which prevents a man earning his daily bread must be worthless.

So in due course he installed himself with an ill grace upon the footpath of Bhendi Bazar with portfolio and inkhorn, writing letters for uneducated Musulmans, petitions for candidates and English accounts for butlers. And the more he wrote the more convinced he became that he was sacrificing himself for a woman who could not realize the measure of his fall. Thus for a time matters remained—little Imtiazan wearing her delicate fingers out at home, he plying his pen in the street,—until one day a dancing-girl from Lucknow called him to her house to write an important missive on her behalf. This chance acquaintance ripened into a friendship that boded no good for Imtiazan: for within a month, amid specious statements of lucrative employment and fair promises of future well-being, he bade her prepare to leave the small room and accompany him to a larger house, fronting a main thoroughfare, which, said he, would henceforth be their home. The sight of the unscreened windows of her new home struck a chill into Imtiazan's heart; and when the door opened and she was met by three elderly Muhammadans who saluted her as their "Bai-Saheb," fear took possession of her soul. The thin red cases hanging on the wall told her that the men were musicians; and in response to the mute appeal in her eyes her husband bade her with almost brutal candour prepare to adopt her old profession of dancing and singing in order to save him from the hateful duties of a public letter-writer.

For two days Imtiazan tended by the musicians and their wives was a prey to the blackest despair, and then deeming it useless to protest, she set herself courageously to do her husband's bidding and to dance as she had danced in the house of Gowhar Jan. But she little knew the true depths of her husband's selfishness. "Money comes not fast enough" was his perpetual cry and he urged her, at first gently but with ever-increasing vehemence, to sink still lower. The memory of the past and who knows what higher instinct helped her to withstand his sordid demands for many days: but at length, realizing that this was *kismet* and tired of the perpetual upbraiding, she consented to do his bidding. So for three weary years the waters closed over Imtiazan. One day she awoke to find that her husband had crowned his villainy by decamping with her valuables and all her savings. She followed and found him, and, pressing into his hand a little extra money that he had in his hurry overlooked, she bade him a bitter farewell for ever. She rested a day or two to get herself properly divorced from him, and then returned alone to the hated life in Bombay.

There Fortune smiled upon her and wealth poured into her lap. Two years later by dint of careful inquiry she discovered that the stern-faced woman who had abandoned her in the Lahore market was her uncle's wife, now widowed and in poverty; and to her she of her bounty gave a pension. For Imtiazan, though she never forgot, could always forgive and had never lost the sense of her duty to relations. She also provided for the old man who had helped her when a child to build the dust-castles beneath the trees of her old home; and then, while still young and with enough money left to keep herself in comparative affluence, she turned her back for ever upon the profession which she loathed and devoted the rest of her life to the careful rearing of an orphan girl, whom the desire for a child of her own and the memories of her own youth urged her to adopt. When she died, the child who had grown up and under her guidance had married a respectable merchant, mourned for her as one mourns for those who have lovingly shielded our infancy and youth; and many of the neighbours were sincerely grieved that Imtiazan had departed for ever.

Such is the life-history of Imtiazan, one of the most famous dancing-girls Bombay has ever known a history that lacks not pathos. After her final renunciation of the profession of singing and dancing she might have remarried and in fact received more than one offer from men who were attracted by her kindliness of heart and by her beauty. But she declined them all with the words "Marriage is not my *kismet,*" which is but the Indian equivalent of "My faith hath departed and my heart is broken." Surely the earth lies very lightly upon Imtiazan.

VI.

# THE BOMBAY MOHURRUM.

## STRAY SCENES.

THE luxury of grief seems common to mankind all the world over, and the mourning of the Mohurrum finds its counterpart in the old lamentation for the slain Adonis, the emotional tale of Sohrab's death at the hand of his sire Rustom, and the long-drawn sorrow of the Christian Passion. The Persian inclination towards the emotional side of human nature was not slow to discover amid the early martyrs of the Faith one figure whose pathetic end was powerful to awaken every chord of human pity. The picture of the women and children of high lineage deceived, deserted and tortured with thirst, of the child's arms lopped at the wrist even at the moment they were stretched forth for the blessing of the Imam, of the noblest chief of Islam betrayed and choosing death to dishonour, of his last lonely onset, his death and mutilation at the hand of a former friend and fellow-champion of the faith,—this picture indeed appealed and still appeals, as no other can, to the hidden depths of the Persian heart. The Sunni may object to the choice of Hasan and Husain as the martyrs most worthy of lamentation, putting forward in their stead Omar, companion of the Prophet himself, who lingered for three days in the agony of death, or Othman, the third Khalifa, who died of thirst, or "the Lion of God," whose life came to so disastrous a close. But the Shia, while admitting that the death of the first martyrs may have wrought severer loss to Islam, cannot admit that their end surpasses in pathos the tale of the bitter tenth of Mohurrum when the stars quivered in a blood-red sky and the very walls of the palace of Kufa rained tears of blood as the head of the Martyr was borne before them. He cannot also approve the Sunni practice of converting a season of mourning into one of revelry and brawl, for he does not realize the influence of the local Hindu element upon the Mohurrum and cannot comprehend that the Indian additions to the festival have their roots in the deep soil of Hindu spirit-belief. For to the Hindu, and to the Sunni Mahomedan who has borrowed somewhat from him, all seasons of death and mourning act as a lode-stone to the unhoused and naked spirits who are ever wandering through the silent spaces of the East. Some of these spirits we can appease or coax into becoming guardian-angels by housing them in handsome cenotaphs; others we can lodge in the horse-shoe or in that great spirit-house, the tiger, letting them sport for a day or two in the bodies of our men and youths, who are adorned with yellow stripes symbolical of their rôle; while other more malevolent spirits can only be driven away by shouting, buffeting and drumming, such as characterize the Mohurrum season in Bombay. The Indian element of nervous excitement might in course of ages have been sobered by the puritanism of Islam but for the presence of the African, who unites with a firm belief in spirits a phenomenal desire for noise and brawling; and it is the union of this jovial African element with the sentimentality of Persia and the spirit-worship of pure Hinduism which renders the Bombay Mohurrum more lively and more varied than any Mahomedan celebration in Cairo, Damascus or Constantinople.

Although the regular Mohurrum ceremonies do not commence until the fifth day of the Mohurrum moon, the Mahomedan quarters of the city are astir on the first of the month. From morn till eve the streets are filled with bands of boys, and sometimes girls, blowing raucous blasts on hollow bamboos, which are adorned with a tin 'panja,'—the sacred open hand emblematical of the Prophet, his daughter Fatima, her husband Ali and their two martyred sons. The sacred five, in the form of the outstretched hand, adorn nearly all Mohurrum symbols, from the toy trumpet and the top of the banner-pole to the horse-shoe rod of the devotee and the 'tazia' or domed bier. Youths, preceded by drummers and clarionet-players, wander through the streets laying all the shop-keepers under contribution for subscriptions; the well-to-do householder sets to building a 'sabil' or charity-fountain in one corner of his verandah or on a site somewhat removed from the fairway of traffic; while a continuous stream of people afflicted by the evil-eye flows into the courtyard of the Bara Imam Chilla near the Nal Bazaar to receive absolution from the peacock-feather brush and sword there preserved. Meanwhile in almost every street where a 'tabut' is being prepared elegiac discourses ('waaz') are nightly delivered up to the tenth of the month by a *maulvi*, who draws from Rs. 30 to Rs. 100 for his five nights' description of the martyrdom of Husain; while but a little distance away boys painted to resemble tigers leap to the rhythm of a drum, and the Arab mummer with the split bamboo shatters the nerves of the passer-by by suddenly cracking it behind his back. The fact that this Arab usually takes up a strong position near a 'tazia' suggests the idea that he must originally have represented a guardian or scapegoat, designed to break by means of his abuse, buffoonery and laughter the spell of the spirits who long for quarters within the rich mimic tomb; and the fact that the crowds who come to gaze in admiration on the 'tazia' never retort or round upon him for the sudden fright or anger that he evokes gives one the impression that the crack of the bamboo is in their belief a potent scarer of unhoused and malignant spirits.

Turn off the main thoroughfare and you may perhaps find a lean Musalman, with a green silk skull-cap, sitting in a raised and well-lighted recess in front of an urn in wich frankincense is burning. He has taken a vow to be a "Dula" or bridegroom during the Mohurrum. There he sits craning his neck over the smoke from the urn and swaying from side to side, while at intervals three companions who squat beside him give vent to a cry of "Bara Imam ki dosti yaro din" (cry "din" for the friendship of the twelve Imams). Then on a sudden the friends rise and bind on to the

Dula's chest a pole surmounted with the holy hand, place in his hand a brush of peacock's feathers and lead him thus bound and ornamented out into the highway. Almost on the threshold of his passage a stout Punjabi Musulman comes forward to consult him. "Away, away" cry the friends "Naya jhar hai" (this is a new tree), meaning thereby that the man is a new spirit-house and has never before been possessed. A little further on the procession, which has now swelled to considerable size, is stopped by a Mahomedan from Ahmednagar who seeks relief. He places his hand upon the Dula's shoulder and asks for a sign. "Repeat the creed," mutters the ecstatic bridegroom. "Repeat the durud" say the Dula's supporters; and all present commence to repeat the "Kalmah" or creed and the "Durud" or blessing. Then turning to the Mahomedan who stopped him, the bridegroom of Husein cries: "Sheikh Muhammad, thou art possessed by a jinn—come to my shrine on Thursday next," and with these words sets forth again upon his wanderings. Further down the Bhendi Bazaar a Deccan Mhar woman comes forward for enlightenment, and the Dula, after repeating the Kalmah, promises that she will become a mother before the year expires; while close to Phulgali a Konkani Musulman woman, who has been possessed for six months by a witch (Dakan), is flicked thrice with the peacock-feather brush and bidden to the Dula's shrine on the following Thursday. So the Dula fares gradually forward, now stopped by a Kunbi with a sick child, now by some Musulman mill-hands, until he reaches the Bismillah shrine, where he falls forward on his face with frothing mouth and convulsed body. The friends help the spirit which racks him to depart by blowing into his ear a few verses of the Koran; whereat the Dula, after a possession of about four hours, regains consciousness, looks around in surprise, and retires to his home fatigued but at last sane.

Wherever a "tazia" or tomb is a-building, there gather all the Mohurrum performers, the Nal Sahebs or Lord Horse-shoes, the tigers and the mummers of Protean disguise. The spot becomes an "Akhada" or tryst at which the tomb-builders entertain all comers with draughts of sherbet or sugared water, but not with betel which has no place in seasons of mourning. Here for example comes a band of Marathas and Kamathis with bells upon their ankles, who form a ring in front of the "tazia", while their leader chants in a loud voice :—

> "Alif se Allah; Be se Bismillah; Jum se meri Jan. Tajun Imam Husein Ki nyaz dharun."
> Alif for Allah; B for Bismillah; J for my life. An offering is this to Husein."

The chorus take up the refrain at intervals accompanying it with the tinkle of the ankle-bells; and then as distant drumming heralds the approach of a fresh party, they repeat the Mohurrum farewell "Ishki Husein" (Love of Husein) and pass away with the answer of the tryst-folk: "Yadi Husein" (Memory of

Husein) still ringing in their ears. The new party is composed of Bombay Musulman youths, the tallest of whom carries an umbrella made out of pink, green and white paper, under which the rest crowd and sing the following couplet relating to the wife and daughter of Husein :—

> "Bano ne Sakinah se kaha. Tum ko khabar hai Baba gae mare!"

> "Bano said unto Sakinah. Have you heard that your father is dead?"

This party in turn yields place to a band of pipers and drummers, accompanying men who whirl torches round their head so skilfully that the eye sees nought but a moving circle of flame; and they are succeeded by Musulman men and boys, disguised as Konkani fishermen and fishwives, who chant elegies to Husein and keep the rhythm by clapping their hands or by swinging to and fro small earthen pots pierced to serve as a lamp. The last troupe, dressed in long yellow shirts and loose yellow turbans, represent Swami Narayan priests and pass in silence before the glittering simulacrum of the Martyr's tomb.

The most curious feature of the Mohurrum celebration is the roystering and brawling of the *Tolis* or street-bands which takes places for two or three nights after the fifth day of the month. Each street has its own band ready to parade the various quarters of the city and fight with the bands of rival streets. If the rivalry is good-humoured, little harm accrues; but if, as is sometimes the case, feelings of real resentment are cherished, heads are apt to be broken and the leaders find themselves consigned to the care of the Police. It is difficult to see the connection between these brawling street-companies and the lamentation for Hasan and Husein; but the rivalry of the *mohollas* recalls the free-fighting which used once to take place between the various quarters of Gujarat and Kathiawar towns during the Holi festival, while the beating, shouting and general pandemonium evoked by the *Tolis* are probably akin to the extravagance once practised at the beating of the bounds in England and Scotland and are primarily designed to scare away evil-spirits from the various quarters of the city. The *Tolis* are indeed a relic of pure Hinduism—of aboriginal spirit-belief, and have in the course of centuries been gradually associated with the great Mahomedan Festival of Tears. Originally they can have had no connection with the Mohurrum and are in essence as much divorced from the lamentation over the slaughter at Karbala as are the mummers, the Nal Sahebs and the Lords of the conchshell ( Sain Kowra ) of the modern celebration from the true Mahomedan who wanders back from the sea-shore uttering the cry of grief—

" Albida, re albida, Ya Huseini albida."

" Farewell, farewell, ah, my Husein, farewell ! "

## VII.

## THE POSSESSION OF AFIZA.

IT was quite evident that something was seriously wrong with Abdulla the Dhobi. His features had lost their former placidity and wore an aspect of troubled wonder; the clothes which he erstwhiles washed and returned to their owners with such regularity were now brought back long after the proper date and occasionally were not returned at all; and the easy good temper which once characterized his conversation had yielded place to sudden outbursts of anger or protracted spells of sulkiness. The major-domo consulted on the point could only suggest that Abdulla's ill-temper was typical of the inherent "badmashi" of the Dhobi nature and that probably Abdulla had taken to nocturnal potations, while the youngest member of the household unhesitatingly laid down that Abdulla had been seized by a "bhut" or in other words was possessed of a devil. When the former suggestion was laid before Abdulla, he contemned it with unmeasured scorn and then turned and rent the spirit of the butler with winged words, but the small boy's opinion seemed to give him pause. He held his peace for a moment, gazing earthwards and rubbing a small heap of dust towards him with his toe; and then on a sudden he burst out into the tale which is here set down in his own words:—

"'Nay, Saheb, I am possessed of no devil, but my wife Afiza is sore troubled by one. Only three months ago I sent for her from my village, as she was expecting to become a mother and I was desirous of looking early upon my first-born child; and for six weeks she dwelt contentedly with me in the house which I have rented near the ghat. And then the child was born—a child without blemish; and Afiza and I were happy. But, Saheb, the shadow of evil was even then drawing nigh unto us. For on the sixth day after birth, when the midwife was about to light the four-wicked lamp for the 'chatti' ceremony, Afiza suddenly cast the child from her, leaped wildly from the couch, tearing at her hair and swaying to and fro as one demented, and broke the lamp with her hands. And the midwife fled from the room crying for help, and brought my mother and my sister in to try and soothe her. And even while they wrestled with her spirit someone set light to the urn of frankincense, for it was the evening of Thursday; and as the thick smoke curled upwards towards Afiza, she trembled and gasped out:—'This is my house; and this woman hath been delivered on the spot where I died in childbirth five years ago! I will never cease troubling her, for she hath forgotten even to burn a little 'loban' (frankincense) for the repose of my spirit.' So saying my wife fell senseless on the ground and remained motionless for thirty minutes until the spirit had fled. And, Saheb, from that day forward not an evening passes but the 'suwandi' (the spirit of a woman who has died in travail) lays hold upon her, and my house has become a place of evil and a byword among the neighbours. Several exorcists, Siyanas and Syeds have we consulted, but all in vain. Their ministrations only make her worse. What can be done !"

One can hardly conjecture the ultimate fate of Abdulla and his family, had not some one who took an interest in the case suggested a final resort to the Syed from Cambay, who some little time ago opened in Goghari street a branch of the famous Gujarat shrine of Miran Datar. To him Abdulla half-hopeful, half-desperate, repaired : and the Syed came into his house and gave Afiza a potion composed of incense-ashes and water from the Miran shrine. But the evil spirit was terribly violent ; and it required regular treatment of this nature for fully twenty days ere it could be dislodged. Evening after evening Afiza was taken into the presence of Syed, who summoned forth the spirit with a drink of the sacrosanct water ; and at home Abdulla and his mother who had been supplied with water and ashes by the Syed, were wont likewise to summon the spirit at any hour which they felt would cause it inconvenience. Thus the struggle between the powers of light and darkness for the soul of Afiza continued, until at length the evil spirit deemed it wise to depart : and on the twenty-first day, when it was racking Afiza for the last time, it demanded as the final price of its departure the liver of a black-goat. So Abdulla hearkened to the spirit's will and buried the pledge of his wife's recovery in a new earthen pot just at the spot where the four roads meet near his house And Afiza was at peace.

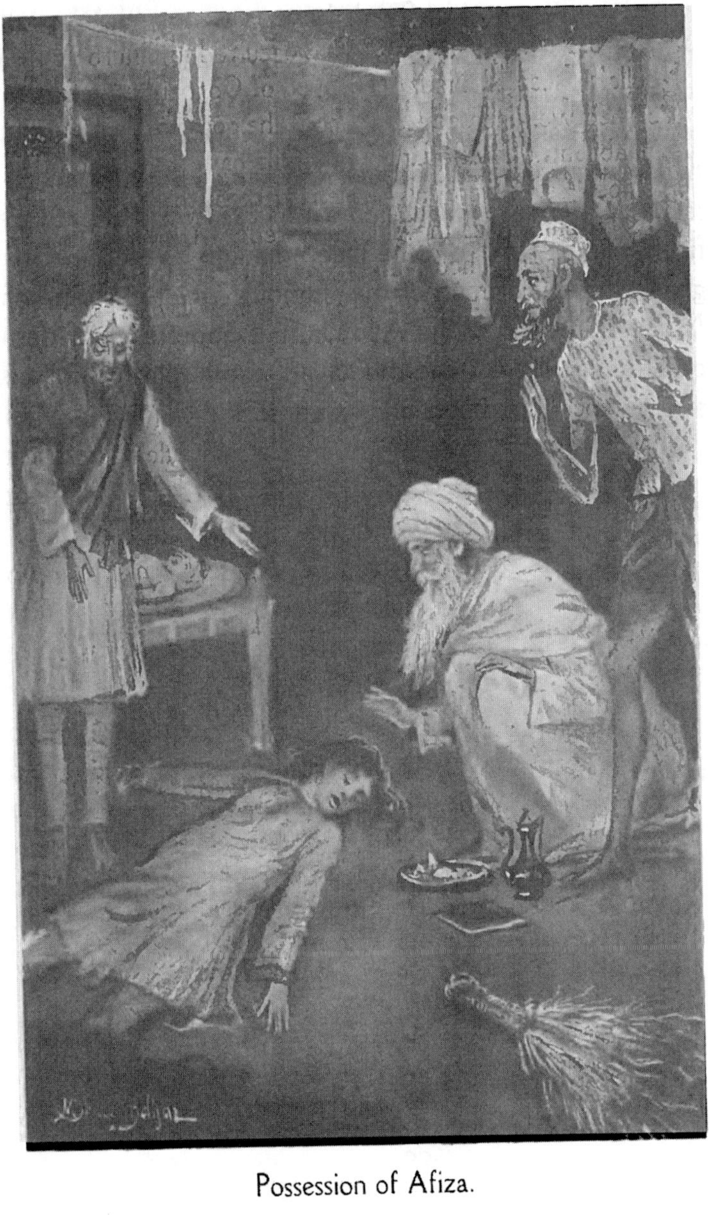

Possession of Afiza.

Since that date nought has occurred to disturb Abdulla's peace of mind. The Syed of Goghari street has earned well-merited fame among the poorer Musulman inhabitants of that quarter; Abdulla has cast off his ill temper as it were a garment; Afiza the possessed has become Afiza the self-possessed, helping Abdulla to earn his livelihood and obtain the approval of his masters; and the child, unharmed by the Evil Eye and beloved of his parents, is daily waxing in favour with God and man. According to Abdulla the only spirit with occasionally attacks him is a spirit of mischief not unknown to the parents of healthy little boys.

VIII.

## A KASUMBA DEN.

WANDER down one of the greatest arteries of the city and you will perhaps notice on the east side of the street a double-storied house bearing all the appearance of prolonged neglect and decay. Enter the low door and take a sharp turn to the right and you will find yourself at length on an ill-smelling landing with a creaking ladder-like staircase in one corner, enveloped from top to bottom in darkness so profound that one can almost conjure up visions of sudden death from the assassin's dagger. After a moment's hesitation you commence to grope your way upwards: the staircase sways and creaks beneath your feet; the air is heavy with strange odours; something,—probably a cat—scuttles past you and nearly upsets your balance; and putting out your hand to steady yourself your fingers touch something clammy and corpselike which turns out to be a Ghati labourer, naked save for a loin-cloth, asleep in the narrow niche between the walls of the ground-floor and the first storey. One wonders what he pays for this precarious accommodation, in which a sudden movement during sleep may mean a sheer drop down the dark staircase. But fortunately he sleeps motionless, like one physically tired out, perchance after dragging bales about the dock sheds since early morn or wandering all day round the city with heavy loads upon his head.

At length on the second storey a half-open door casts an arrow of light upon your path. You hail it with joy after the Cimmerian gloom of the lower floors; and, pushing the door further ajar, you find yourself in a square low room lit by two windows which command a view of the street below. It is carpeted with cheap date-leaf mats and a faded polychrome "dhurri"; dirty white cushions are propped against the wall below the windows; a few square desk-like boxes lie in front of the cushions; and in a semi-recumbent attitude around the room are some 20 or 30 men—Bombay and Gujarat Mahomedans, men from Hindustan and one or two Daudi Bohras, the regular customers of the "Kasumba" saloon. There is one woman in the room—a member of the frail sisterhood, now turned faithful, nursing an elderly and peevish Lothario with a cup of sago-milk gruel, which opium-eaters consider such a delicacy: while the other customers sit in groups talking with the preternatural solemnity born of their favourite drug, and now and again passing a remark to the cheery-looking landlord with the white skull-cap and henna-tinged beard.

Each occupant of the room has been provided with a tiny glass of weak opium-water from the large China jar on the landlord's desk, paying a pice per glass for the beverage. Some drink one glass, some two, some three or more; but as a rule the "kasumba" drinker confines himself to two glasses, being ashamed to own even to a brother "Tiryaki" the real quantity of the drug consumed by him: while a few, strengthened by prolonged habit, pay somewhat more than the ordinary price for a thicker and stronger dilution. When the glasses are empty the company calls for desert; for the opium-drinker must always have his "*kharbhanjan*" or bitter taste remover; and the landlord straightway produces sweets, fruit, parched gram, or sago-gruel known as "*khir*" according to the taste of his customers. Hardly has dessert ended when an elderly Mahomedan in shabby garb falls out of the group and clearing his throat to attract attention commences to recite a flowery prelude in verse. He is the "Dastan-Shah," own brother (professionally) of the "Sammar" or story-teller of Arabia and the "Shayir" of Persia and Cairo: and his stories, which he delivers in a quaint sing-song fashion, richly interspersed with quotations from the poets of Persia, are usually culled from the immortal "Thousand and one Nights" or are concerned with the exploits and adventures of one of the great heroes of Islam. Amir-Hamza for example is a favourite subject of the imaginative eastern story-teller. Amir-Hamza according to Professor Dryasdust died before the Prophet, but according to the Troubadours of Islam was the hero of a thousand stirring deeds by flood and field and by the might of his right hand converted to the Faith the Davs and the Peris of Mount Kaf (the Caucasus). You will hear, if you care to, of his resourceful and trusty squire Umar Ayyar, owner of the magic "zambil" or satchel which could contain everything, and master of a rude wit, similar to that of Sancho Panza, which serves as an agreeable contrast to the somewhat ponderous chivalry of the knight-errant of Islam.

Thus the Dastan-Shah whiles away time until about 8 p. m. when the club breaks up and the faded Aspasia helps her fractious Pericles down the rotten staircase and out into the night. Ere the company departs each member subscribes a pice for the story-teller, who in this way earns about forty pice a day,-no inconsiderable income in truth for the mere retail of second-hand fables: and then with a word of peace to the landlord the men troop slowly forth to their homes. As we pass down the rotten staircase, lit this time for our benefit with a moribund cocoanut oil lamp, we mark the Maratha labourer still sleeping heavily in his niche, dreaming perhaps amid the heavy odours of the house of the fresh wind-swept uplands of his Deccan home.

# IX.

## THE GANESH CAVES.

FIFTY-SIX miles to the north of Poona lies the old town of Junner, which owing to its proximity to the historic Nana Ghat was in the earliest times an important centre of trade. As early as 100 years before the birth of Christ, the Nana Pass was one of the chief highways of trade between Aparantaka or the Northern Konkan and the Deccan; and although the steep and slippery nature of the ascent must have prevented cart-traffic, the number of pack-bullocks and ponies that were annually driven upwards towards the cooler atmosphere and richer soil of Junner must have been considerable. Once the Nana Ghat had been crossed the traveller found himself in a land marked out by Nature herself for sojourn and settlement: for there lay before his eyes a fruitful plain, well-shaded, well-watered and girt with mighty hills of rock, which needed but the skill of man to be transformed into a chain of those "Viharas" or places of rest and recreation, which the Buddhists of pre-Christian and early Christian ages sought to establish. Thus it happens that in each of the mountain ranges which rise around Junner are found caves and shrines hewn out of the solid rock by the followers of Buddhism, some with inscriptions in obsolete characters and all of them in a wonderful state of preservation, considering the ages that have passed since their foundation.

Among those most easy of access are the Ganesh Lena, as they are called hollowed out of the vast rounded scarp, which rising a hundred feet above the plain projects from the Hatkeshvar and Suleman ranges about a mile northward of the town. A fairly smooth but dusty road leads the traveller down to the Kukdi river dried by the fair weather into stagnant pools, in which the women wash their clothes and the buffaloes lounge heavily, and thence through garden-land and clumps of mango-trees to the under-slopes of the mountain. There the road proper merges into a rocky pathway, which in turn yields place some little distance further on to a series of well-laid masonry steps, of comparatively recent date, which, as they curve upwards, recall to one's mind the well-known Hundred Steps at Windsor Castle. The steps are divided into about ten flights, and are said to have been built at different times by devotees of God Ganesh in gratitude for his having granted their prayers. What prompted the first worshipper to prove his gratitude in this form none can say: he might have so easily satisfied his conscience with a presentation to the God or by the erection of a small shrine in the plains. But happily for all men he adopted the more philanthropic course of smoothing the road to the presence of the kindly Deity. Others, the recipients of like favours and fired by his example, added each in their turn to the work, until the once rude track was transformed into a massive stone-approach fit for the feet of princes.

The caves are twenty-six in number and consist mainly of dwellings and cells, with three water-cisterns two of which bear inscriptions. and a chapel. The cells are all hewn into somewhat similar pattern and shape, containing on one and sometimes two sides long stone benches, which served doubtless as the resting-place of their Buddhist occupants. The " Chaitya Vihara " or chapel cave alone is worth a visit. Pillars and pilasters with eight-sided shafts and waterpot-bases, which scholars attribute to the period B. C. 90 to A, D. 300, stand sentinel over verandahs stretching away into darkness on either side of the main aisle. Their capitals are surmounted with crouching animals, twin elephants, a sphinx and lion, twin tigers, all beautifully carved through in places broken ; while above them the main walls of the cave rise steep into a pointed vault, the centre of which is some twenty-four feet from the ground-floor. The relic-shrine or "Daghoba" at the far end of the chapel stands upon a high plinth, and is crowned by a rounded dome, similar to the "Daghoba" at Vyaravali which overlooks the dead city of Pratappur in Salsette. One of the members of our party struck the plinth with a *dhotar* to awaken the echoes which eddy loudly round the vault and rouse the wild birds that have built their nests in the holes and cornices. The birds as well as the bats which lurk in the darker recesses of the chapel are said to be responsible for the very pungent and unpleasant odour which greets one on entering and forces one to cut short one's visit. And what of him who built the shrine? Deep in the back wall of the verandah is graven, in characters long since obsolete, an inscription interpreted some time ago by scholars, which tells how Sulasadata, the illustrious son of Heranika of Kalyana, presented the chapel to the monastery, to the glory of God and his own lasting merit. The rock-hewn words are headed and ended with the "Swastika" or symbol of good fortune, which appears in so many messages from Buddhist ages.

On the left of the chapel at a slightly higher level stands the largest of this group of caves, a large hall with a verandah and twenty cells around it. Later ages have converted the whole cave into a temple of Ganpati, whence the caves obtain their name of Ganesh Lena; and the once plain walls, whose very austerity reflected perhaps the life of the monks dwelling within them, have been rudely plastered, white-washed and covered with inferior representations of incidents in the lives of Devi, Krishna, Shiv and Ganpati. In the centre of the back wall, between two ancient stone seats, glowers a rude "eidolon," aflame with red lead and *ghi*, so thickly smeared indeed that the original features and form of the god have well-nigh disappeared. Yet this is Ganesh, the kindly Ganesh, who turns not a deaf ear to the prayers of his servants and in whose honour the stone steps were hewn and laid. Two *pujaris* of the Yajurvedi Brahman stock and three or four women, who are attached to the shrine, crave alms for the God. They and their forbears, they tell you, have been the officiating priests for years; wherefore, desirous of testing their knowledge, you enquire who built these mighty dwelling-places. "Hindus of a thousand years ago," say they, "who desired to acquire merit." But ask the untutored villager who has guided you up the hill ; and straightway comes the answer; —"Sahib, these were not built by man, but by the Gods ere man came hither !"

Outside the cave is a pleasant verandah and balustrade, whence you look down over the bare lower slopes to the garden-studded course of the river. Beyond lies a long low trail of vapour, which marks the position of Junner, and behind that again climb heaven-ward the Manmoda hills. On the right, with its ruined mosque and conning-tower grey in the morning light, the massive pile of Shivner frowns over the valley, like some dismasted battleship, hurled upwards into sudden petrifaction by the hands of Titans. It is an impressive scene—the pre-Christian monastery behind you; the relics of Musulman and Maratha sovereignty in front; and below, bathed in a sea of morning-mist which Surya is hastening to disperse, Junner, the town of ancient memories, in her latest *avatar* of a British Taluka Headquarter station. Let us hope that the monuments which we raise will last as long as those of Buddhist monk or Mahomedan Killedar.

X.

# A BHANDARI MYSTERY.

IN the heart of the great palm-groves to the north-west of Dadar lies an "oart" known as Borkar's Wadi, shaded by tall well-tended trees whose densely-foliaged summits ward off the noon-day sun and form a glistening screen at nights, what time the moon rises full-faced above the eastern hills. Not very long ago, at a time when cholera had appeared in the city and was taking a daily toll of life, this oart was the scene of a bi-weekly ceremony organized by the Bhandaris of Dadar and Mahim and designed to propitiate the wrath of the cholera-goddess, who had slain several members of that ancient and worthy community. For the Bhandaris, be it noted, know little of western theories of disease and sanitation; and such precautions as the boiling of water, even were there time to boil it, and abstention from fruit seem to them utterly beside the mark and valueless, so long as the goddess of cholera, Jarimari, and the thirty-eight Cholera Mothers are wroth with them. Thus at the time we speak of, when many deaths among their kith and kin had afforded full proof that the goddess was enraged, they met in solemn conclave and decided to perform every Sunday and Tuesday night for a month such a ceremony as would delight the heart of that powerful deity and stave off

A Bhandari Mystery.

further mortality. The limitation of the period of propitiation to one month was based not so much upon religious grounds as upon the fact that a Municipality, with purely Western ideas of sanitation and of combating epidemics, refused to allow the maintenance of the shed, which was to be the temporary home of Jarimari, for more than thirty days. Yet it matters but little, this time-limit: for a month is quite long enough for the complete assuagement of the anger of one who, though proverbially capricious, is by no means unkindly.

Let us glance at the ceremony as performed on a Tuesday night towards the middle of the month of propitiation. In the darkest portion of the *wadi* stands a rude hut, containing the emblems of the Mother, occupied for the time being by Rama Bhandari, who acts as a species of medium between the goddess and his kinsmen. In front of the hut a space has been cleared and levelled, flanked on one side by mats for the Bhandari musicians, singers, drummers and cymbal-players, and on the other by four or five chairs and a few wooden benches for the initiates in the mysteries; and to the stems of several neighbouring trees lamps have been affixed about five feet from the ground, which cast weird shadows across the threshold of the goddess's home. Rama, the high-priest of this woodland rite—a dark, thin man with a look of anxiety upon his face—enters the hut with his assistant, Govind, while several fresh looking Bhandari boys take up their position near the gong, cymbals, and drum, prepared when the hour comes to hammer them with might and main. A pause—and Rama returns bearing the symbol or idol of the Mother, followed by Govind carrying a lighted saucer-lamp. The idol, for such we must perforce style it, is nothing more nor less than a bright brass pot, full of water, set on a wooden stool which is thickly covered with flowers. In the mouth of the water-pot rests a husked cocoanut, with a hole in the upper end into which are thrust the stems of a bouquet of jasmine, with long arms of jasmine hanging down on either side. Now the water-pot is the shrine, the very home of Jarimari and the thirty-eight cholera mothers. Behind the jasmine-wreathed stool Govind places another stool bearing a tin tray full of uncooked rice, camphor, and black and red scented powder; and close to it he piles the cocoanuts, sugar, camphor, cakes, betel-nuts, and marigolds which the Bhandari initiates have sent as an offering to Rama. He next produces a pile of incense-sprinkled cinders, which he places in front of the goddess, and several incense-cones which he lights, while Rama lays down a handful of light canes for use at the forthcoming ceremony. And while the rich scented smoke rises in clouds into the still night-air, shrouding the goddess's face, Govind takes a little rice from the tray and a few flowers, and places them on a Tulsi or sweet basil shrine which stands a little northward of the hut.

All is now ready. Rama bids the boys sound the note of gathering, and at once such a clashing and drumming arises as would frighten all the devils of the palm-groves. The people come but slowly, for many of them work late in the mills and have to go home and cook and eat their evening-meal before they can take part in the rites of the Mother. But at last groups of women appear out of the darkness, bareheaded save for flower-wreaths and a few gold ornaments, their saris wound tightly round waist and shoulder. They cluster silent and close-packed round the door of the hut; for they are the women whom the thirty-eight Mothers love to possess and to lash into the divine frenzy which only the human form can adequately portray. Govind stirs the incense-heap; the dense smoke rolls forth again and shrouds all; there is a feeling of witchery in the air and in the midst of the smoke-pall one can just descry Rama bending low before the Mother. Now he rises, draws the rattan-canes through his hands, and then leans against a palm-tree with eyes tightly closed and hands quivering as if in pain. But hark! there is something toward in the hut, and out of the darkness dash two young women right in front of the goddess, leaping and tossing their arms. They sway and twist their lithe forms in the smoke but utter no word. Only one can see their breasts heaving beneath the sari and can catch the sharp "Hoo, hoo" of their breathing, as their frenzy heightens. Now from the other end of the hut two more rush forth, staggering, towards the Tulsi shrine, and after the same mad gyrations dance towards the Mother and bury their heads in the smoke; and they are followed at momentary intervals by others who fly, some to the Tulsi shrine, others to the Goddess but all mad with frenzy, dancing, leaping, swaying, until they sink overpowered by fatigue. Meanwhile Rama is performing a devil dance of his own in the smoke-clouds; the gong is ringing, cymbals clashing, onlookers shouting; the tresses of the women have fallen down and in the half-light look like black snakes writhing in torture; the women themselves are as mad as the Bacchantes and Menads of old fable: in a word, it is Pandemonium let loose!

The noise ebbs and flows, now dying down as the first frenzy fades away, now rising more shrill as the spirit of the Mother wracks her devotees more fiercely. That tall finely-formed young woman, who dances like a puppet without will and who never seems to tire, is Moti, leader of the dancers and the favourite choice of Jarimari. There behind her is Ganga, the slightly-built, beloved of Devi, and in the midst of the smoke, swaying frog-like, is Godavari, lashed to madness by Mother Ankai. Around them dance by twos and threes the rest of the women with dishevelled locks and loosened robes, whom Rama taps from time to time with his cane whenever they show signs of giving in. But at length Nature reasserts her sway, and the dancers one and all crouch down in the smoke, their dark sides heaving painfully in the dim light like the implements of some ghostly forge. Now Govind appears again with a tray and marks the brows of the women with a finger-tip of vermilion, his own brow being marked by them in turn. He places a cake of camphor on the tray and sets light to it; and as the clear flame bursts forth in front of the Mother, the whole congregation rises and shouts "Devi ki Jaya" (Victory to the Goddess). Then Moti takes the tray and, balancing it on her head, dances slowly with long swinging stride round the Mother, while the music bursts out with renewed vigour, urging the other women, the human tabernacles of the cholera deities, to follow suit. Thereafter the camphor-cake is handed round to both women and men in turn who plunge their hands in the ashes and smear their faces with them; and so, after distribution of the offering of cocoanuts, sugar, and betel, the celebration closes. A few girls still dance and jerk their shining bodies before the altar, but Rama who is getting weary touches them with his hands, commanding the frenzy to cease, and with a sigh they withdraw one by one into the dark shadows of the palm-grove.

Such is in brief the ceremony of propitiation of the Cholera-Goddess. What does it signify? It appears that according to Bhandari belief the disease is the outcome of neglect of the Mother. The present conditions of life in the cramped and fetid chawls of the city, the long hours of work necessitated by higher rentals and a higher standard of living, leave her devotees but little leisure for her worship. She is maddened by neglect and in revenge she slays her ten or fifteen in a night. Yet is she not by nature cruel. Fashion for her a pleasant shrine, flower-decked, burn incense before her, beat the drum in her honour, let the women offer themselves as the sport and play-thing of her madness and of a surety will she repent her of the evil she hath done and will stay the slaughter. In spirit-parlance a woman chosen by the spirit, into whom as into a shrine the mother enters, is known as a "Jhad" or tree: for just as a tree yields rustling and quivering to the lightest breath of the gale, bends its head and moves its branches to and fro, so the women, losing all consciousness of self, play as the breath of the Mother stirs them, quivering beneath her gentler gusts, bending their bodies and tossing their arms beneath the stronger blasts, and casting themselves low with bowed heads and streaming hair as the full force of the storm enwraps them. They are in very truth as trees shaken by the wind. Nay more, the Mother herself once lived in human form: she knows the pleasure, the comforts of the body and she is fain, by entering the bodies of her female devotees, to renew the memories and suggestions of her former life.

In conclusion one may briefly record what the Bhandaris thought of the presence of a European at their sacred rite. Some feared him as one that contemplated the imposition of a new tax; others viewed him askance as a doctor from the Hospital despatched by higher authority to put an end to the ceremony; and yet others,—the larger number insooth,—deemed that here at last was a Saheb who had found physic a failure and had learned that the Mother alone has power to allay grievous sickness.

# XI.

## SCENES IN BOMBAY.

### A MUSULMAN HOLIDAY.

NEARLY all the Mahomedan inhabitants of Bombay observe as a general picnic day the last Wednesday of the month of 'Safar' which is known as 'Akhiri Char Shamba' or 'Chela Budh'; for on this day the Prophet, convalescent after a severe illness, hied him to a pleasance on the outskirts of Mecca. During the greater portion of the previous night the women of the house are astir, preparing sweetmeats and salt cakes, tinging their hands with henna, bathing and donning new clothes and ornaments; and when morning comes, all Mahomedans, rich and poor, set forth for the open grounds of Malabar Hill, Mahalakshmi, Mahim or Bandora, the Victoria Gardens, or the ancient shrine of Mama Hajiyani (Mother Pilgrim) which crowns the north end of the Hornby Vellard. To the Victoria Gardens the tram cars bring hundreds of holiday-makers, most of whom remain in the outer or free zone of the gardens and help to illumine its grass plots and shady paths with the green, blue, pink and yellow glories of their silk attire. Here a group of men and women are enjoying a cold luncheon; there a small party of Memons are discussing affairs over their 'bidis,' while on all sides are children playing with the paper toys, rattles and tin wheels which the hawkers offer at such seasons of merry-making. Coal-black Africans, ruddy Pathans and yellow Bukharans squat on the open turf to the west of the Victoria and Albert Museum; Mughals in long loose coats and white arch-fronted turbans wander about smoking cigars and chatting volubly, while Bombay Memons in gold turbans or gold-brocade skull-caps, embroidered waistcoats and long white shirts stand on guard over their romping children.

The road leading from Mahalakshmi to the shrine of Mama Hajiyani is particularly gay, and the Vellard is lined throughout its entire length with carriages full of men, women and children in their finest attire; while under the palms on the east side of the road the hum of a great crowd is broken from time to time by the cry of the sellers of sweets, toasted gram, parched pistachio nuts and salted almonds, or by the chink of the coffee seller's cups. A happy, orderly crowd it is, free from all signs of quarrelling and excess, packed more densely than usual around the shrine of Mama Hajiyani, where every little vacant space is monopolised by merry-go-rounds and by the booths of bakers and pastry-sellers. Here are men playing cards; others are flying kites; many are thronging the tea, coffee, and cold drink stalls; while in the very heart of the crowd wander Jewish, Panjabi and Hindustani dancing-girls, who have driven hither in hired carriages to display their beauty and their jewels. Mendicants elbow one at every step,—

Mahomedan and Jewish beggars and gipsy-like Wagri women from North Gujarat, who persistently turn a deaf ear to the "Maf-karo" or "Pardon" of those whom they persecute for alms.

Many of the holiday-makers carry packets of basil leaves and flowers, which they place upon the grave of the Mother Pilgrim, silently repeating as they do so the Fatiha' or prayers for the dead. Others more Puritanical, perchance more sceptical, utter not their prayers to the grave; but as the words pass their lips, turn their faces seawards, remembering Holy Mecca in the far west. Glance for a minute within the room that enshrines the tomb, and you will see the walls hung with tiny toy cradles, —the votive offerings of heartsick women from whom the grace of Mama Hajiyani has lifted the curse of childlessness. So, as the sun sinks, you pass back from the peace of the Mother Pilgrim's grave to the noise of the holiday-making crowd; and turning homewards you hear above you the message of the green parrakeets skimming towards the tomb "like a flight of emerald arrows stolen from the golden quiver of the Twilight."

## A BOMBAY MOSQUE.

Who does not know the Mahomedan quarters of the city of Bombay, with their serried ranks of many-storeyed mansions extending as far as eye can reach?

Dark and forbidding seem many of these houses; and to few is it given to know the secrets they enshrine. But these square battalions of brick and plaster are not wholly continuous. For here and there the ranks are broken by the plain guard-wall and deep-eaved porch, or by the glistening domes and balcony-girt minarets of a mosque: and at such points one may, if one so wish, see more of the people who dwell in the silent houses than one could hope to see during the course of a month's peregrinations up and down the streets devoted to the followers of the Prophet.

Stand with me at sundown opposite the gateway of the mosque and watch the stream of worshippers flowing in through the portals of the house of prayer. Here are the rich purse-proud merchants of Persia, clad in their long black coats; there the full-bearded Maulavis. Behind them come smart sepoys hailing from Northern India, golden-turbaned, shrewd-eyed Memon traders and ruddy-complexioned close-bearded Jats from Multan. Nor is our friend the dark Sidi wanting to the throng: and he is followed by the Arab with his well-known head-gear, by the handsome Afghan, and by the broad-shouldered native of Bokhara in his heavy robes. Mark too the hurried steps of the brocade-worker from Surat, and note the contrast of colour as the grimy fitter or black-smith passes through the porch side by side with the spotlessly-clad Konkani Musulman, whose high features and olive skin betray his Indo-Arab origin. Rich and poor, clean and unclean, all pass in to prayer. As the concourse increases the shoes of the Faithful gather in heaps along the inner edge of the porch : only the newer shoes are permitted to lie, sole against sole, close to their owners, each of whom after washing in the shaded cistern takes his place in the hindmost line of worshippers.

As the service proceeds the ranks of the congregation kneel, stand, fall prostrate, and press the brow upon the ground with a rhythm so reverential and so dignified that the watcher forgets for a time the torn or tawdry raiment, the grime of the factory, the dust of the streets, and feels that each fresh attitude of devotion is indeed the true posture of prayer. It is as a sea troubled by the breath of some unseen spirit, wave upon wave rising, bending, and finally casting itself low in humility and self-sacrifice at the very footstool of the Most High. But all the worshippers are men. "Where are the women," you ask ; "do they not repeat the daily prayers also?" "Verily yes," replies our guide ; "they are all praying in their homes at this hour. More regular, more reverent are they than we are ; and if we men but prayed as the women pray, no shadow would dim the brightness of Islam."

As the evening-prayer progresses groups of men and women with children in their arms gather at the main entrance of the mosque. For the children are vexed with sickness against which medicine has availed nought, and in a higher healing lies their only chance of recovery. So, as the congregation passes out through the gateway, the parents hold

An Arab.

out their ailing children ; and well-nigh every worshipper, rich or poor, young or old, turning his face downwards lets his prayer-laden breath pass over the face of the sick child that needs his aid. A picturesque custom is this, which illustrates two ancient and universal beliefs, namely that all disease is spirit-caused and that the holy book is charm-laden. He who repeats the inspired words of the Koran is purged of all evil, and his breath alone, surcharged with the utterances of divinity, has power to cast out the devils of sickness. Thus to this day all classes of Mahomedans, but particularly the lower classes, carry their sick children to the mosques to receive the prayer-laden breath of the Musallis ( prayer-sayers ): and sometimes in cases of grievous disease a Pir or Mashaikh is asked to perform the healing office, prefacing the brief ceremony with that famous verse of the Koran:—" Wa nunaz-zilo minal Kuraani ma huwa Shifaun wa rah matun lil moaminina" which being interpreted means, " We send down from the Koran that which is a cure and a mercy unto true believers. " So the mosques of the City are homes of healing as well as of prayer.

Occasionally, when the prayer-breath of the ordinary worshipper has failed to effect a cure, a Mussulman mother will take her sick child to some Syed or other holy man in the city for what she calls " Jhada dalwana " ( *i. e.* the sweeping-over ). The Syed questions her about the symptoms and duration of the disease. " Ay me, " moans the mother, " I cannot say what ails the child, Syed Saheb ! He was full of life and health till the other day when I left him on the threshold sucking a sweetmeat. There came by an old Wagri woman who stared at him, whining for alms. I gave her a little bread, wishing her well away : but alack ! no sooner had she gone than my child sickened and hath not recovered since." The Syed then asks her to drop a pice upon a paper covered with magic squares ; which being done, he consults a thumb-marked manuscript and decides that the child is a victim of the Evil Eye. Accordingly he proceeds to pass the end of a twisted handkerchief seven times over the child's body, murmuring at the same time certain mystic formulæ which he, as it were, blows over the child from head to foot. This operation is performed daily for three or four days ; after which in many cases the child actually gets better, and the mother in gratitude pays the Syed from eight annas to a rupee for his kind offices. So too it is the Syed and the prayers he breathes which exorcise the spirit of hysteria that so often lays hold of young maidens ; and it is likewise the prayer-laden breath of the devout man which fortifies the souls of them that have journeyed unto the turnstiles of Night.

# XII.

# CITIZENS OF BOMBAY.

## THE MEMON AND RANGARI.

WOULD you learn how the Memon and the Rangari—two of the most notable inhabitants of the city—pass the waking hours? They are early risers as a rule and are ready to repair to the nearest mosque directly the Muezzin's call to prayer breaks the silence of the approaching dawn, and when the prayers are over they return to a frugal breakfast of bread soaked in milk or tea and then open their shops for the day's business. If his trade permits it, the middle-class Memon will himself go a-marketing, taking with him a "jambil" or Arab-made basket of date-leaves in which to place his vegetables, his green spices, his meat and a little of such fruit as may be in season. His other requisites,—flour, pulse, sugar and molasses,—come to him in what he calls his "khata."—his account with a neighbouring retail-dealer. He is by no means beloved of the Bombay shop-keeper, for he is strict in his observance of the "sunna" which bids him haggle "till his forehead perspires, just as it did in winning the money". The Bombay shop-keeper commences by asking an exorbitant price for his commodi-

A Bombay Memon.

ties; our Memon retorts by offering the least they could possibly fetch; and the battle between the maximum and the minimum eventually settles itself somewhere about the golden mean, whereupon the Memon hies him homewards as full of satisfaction as Thackeray's Jew. In many cases the mother of the house or the sister, if old, widowed and in the words of the Koran "despairing of a marriage," performs the business of shopping and proves herself no less adept than her kinsman at driving a bargain.

About mid-day the Memon or Rangari has his chief meal consisting of leavened or unleavened bread, meat curry or stew or two "kababs" or fried fish, followed perhaps by mangoes, when in season; and when this is over he indulges in a siesta whenever his business allows of it. The afternoon prayers are followed by re-application to business, which keeps him busy in his shop until 8 or 9 p. m., when he again returns home to a frugal supper of "khichdi." It is hardly a satisfying meal, and many young Memons indulge in a fresh collation before retiring to rest. The "khichdi" finished, the young members of the family set forth for their evening resorts, nor forbear to take such refreshment as the city offers on their journey. They purchase a glass of ice-cream here, accept a cup of tea offered by a friend there or purchase a tumbler of "faludah," which plays the same part in the Mahomedan life of Bombay as macaroni does in the life of the Neapolitan. It consists of rice-gruel, cooked and allowed to cool in large copper-trays and sold at the corners of Mahomedan streets. On receiving a demand, the Faludah-seller cuts out a slice from the seemingly frozen mass, puts it into a large tumbler mixes sugar and sherbet with it, and then hands it to his customer who swallows the mixture with every sign of deep satisfaction. If possessed of a conveyance the middle-class Memon will drive about sunset to the Apollo Bunder, Breach Candy or the Bandstand. Happy possessor of a tolerably decent horse and victoria, he considers himself above the conventionalities of dress, and thus may be seen in the skull-cap, waistcoat, long white shirt and trousers which constitute his shop or business-attire, attended not infrequently by little miniatures of himself in similar garb. Reaching the Bunder he silences the importunity of the children by a liberal purchase of salted almonds and pistachios or gram fried in oil, and passes an hour or so in discussing with a friend the market-rate of grain, cotton, *ghi*, or indigo.

If young, the middle-class Memon and Rangari is fond of the native theatres where he rewards Parsi histrionic talent by assiduous attention and exclamations of approval. He and his friends break their journey home by a visit to an Irani or Anglo-Indian soda-water shop, where they repeat the monotonous strain of the theatre songs and assure themselves of the happiness of the moment by asking one another again and again :— "Kevi majha' (what bliss !) to which comes the reply "Ghani majha" or "sari majha"(great bliss !). Then perhaps, if the night is still young, they will knock up the household of a singer and demand a song or two from her. Phryne cannot refuse, however late the hour may be, but she has her revenge by charging a very high price for her songs, which her "ustads" or musicians take care to pocket beforehand. Home is at length reached, and there after a final supper of "malai ke piyale" (cups of cream) and hard-boiled eggs the young Memon disappears until the morrow. The older and more settled members of the community amuse themselves till mid-night by congregating in the tea and coffee shops of the city and there discussing the general trend of trade. Others have formed unions, which assemble at the house of each member in turn and spend a few hours in singing the "maulud" or hymns on the birth of the Prophet (upon whom be peace). These hymns, in pure Hejazi verse, are sung in different measures and are not unpleasant to the ear at a distance. Another peculiar Memon custom is the street-praying for rain. A number of men and boys assemble about 9 p. m., in the street and sing chants set to music by some poet of Gujarat or Hindustan. The chants are really prayers to God for rain, for forgiveness of sins and for absolution from ingratitude for former bounties. One with a strong voice sings the recitative, and then the chorus breaks in with the words "Order, O Lord, the rain-cloud of thy mercy!" Thus chanting the company wanders from street to street till midnight and continues the practice nightly until the rain falls.

A Rangari betrothal though simple enough in itself contains certain elements of interest. The father of the bride-groom usually informs the Patel of the caste that his son's betrothal will take place on a certain day, and on the evening of that day the bridegroom's retinue, accompanied by the Patel and various friends and relations, journeys to the house of the bride. After the company has fully assembled someone brings forward a cocoanut on a tray with a few copper coins beside it. The Patel then asks why the cocoanut has been brought, to which one of the bride's supporters replies "It is for the betrothal of the daughter of Zeid with Omar." This feature of the ceremony is obviously of Hindu origin and must be a legacy of the days when the Rangaris, not yet converted to Islam, belonged to the Hindu Khatri or Kshattriya caste of Gujarat and Cutch. For the loose copper coins, which till recently were styled "dharam-paisa," must be lingering remnants of the Brahman "dakshina," which always accompanied the "shripal" or auspicious fruit; while among Hindus from the very earliest ages cocoanuts have been sent by the bride to the bridegroom, sometimes as earnest of an offer of marriage, sometimes in token of acceptance. After this ceremony is complete the parties cannot retract, the ceremony being considered equivalent to a "nikah" or actual registration by the Kazi; and this fact again discovers the Hindu origin of the Mahomedan Rangaris and of their customs, for among foreign Musulmans the betrothal is a mere period of probation and is terminable at the desire of either party. The "dharam-paisa" usually finds its way into the pocket of the street-Mulla, who has a room in the neighbouring mosque and is charged with the circulation of invitations to all members of the Rangari jamat to assemble at the bride-groom's house for the betrothal-ceremony.

# XIII.

# THE SIDIS OF BOMBAY.

## AN AFRICAN REEL.

AMONG the most curious of the modern portions of Bombay City one may reckon Madanpura, which lies off Ripon Road and is commonly known as the home of the Julhais or Muhammadan weavers from Northern India. It is a rapidly growing quarter, for new chals and new shops spring up every year and quickly find a full complement of tenants from among the lower classes of the population. Amongst those who like the Julhais have moved northward from the older urban area are the Sidis or Musulmans of African descent, who supply the steamship companies with stokers, firemen and engine-room assistants, and the dockyards and workshops with fitters and mechanics. A hardy race they are, with their muscular frames, thick lips and crisp black hair—the very last men you would wish to meet in a rough-and-tumble, and yet withal a jovial people, well-disposed and hospitable to anyone whom they regard as a friend. If they trust you fully they will give you *carte blanche* to witness one of their periodical dances, in which both sexes participate and, which commencing about 10-30 p. m., usually last until 3 or 4 o'clock the following morning. They are worth seeing once, if only for the sake of learning how the Sidis amuse themselves when the spirit moves them.

Imagine a bare white-washed room, opening directly upon the street, the walls of which boast of no ornament save a row of tom-toms, and the sides and window ledges of which are lined with an expectant crowd of Sidis of varying age, from the small boy of eight years to the elderly headman or patel, who is responsible for the good behaviour of the community and is the general arbiter of their internal disputes. This is the Sidi Jamatkhana or caste-hall: and long before you reach the door threading your way through a crowd of squatting hawkers, your ears are assailed by the most deafening noise, reminding you forcibly of the coppersmith's bazaar with an accompaniment of rythmic drumming. The cause is not far to seek. In the centre of the room two Sidis are sitting, in cock-horse fashion, astride what appear to be wooden imitations of a cannon and beating the parchment-covered mouths of their pseudo-steeds with their hands; at their feet a third Sidi is playing a kind of *reveille* upon a flattened kerosine oil-tin; and in the corner, with his back to the audience, an immense African – an ebony Pan blowing frenzy through his wide lips—is forcing the whole weight of his lungs into a narrow reed pipe. The noise is phenomenal, overpowering, but is plainly attractive to Sidi ears; for the room is rapidly filling, and more than one of the spectators suddenly leaps from his seat and circles round the drummers, keeping time to the rythm with queer movements of his body and feet and whirling a "lathi" round his head in much the same fashion as the proverbial Irishman at Donneybrook Fair.

Meanwhile there is some movement toward in the half-light of the inner room. From time to time you catch a glimpse of the black sphinx-faces, immobile and heavy-eyed, framed in scarves bearing a bold pattern of red monkeys and blue palm-trees: and as the din increases the owners of those inscrutable faces creep out and sink down upon a strip of china matting on the far side of the room. They are the wives and daughters of the community some of them young and, from the Sidi point of view, good to look upon, others emulating the elephant in bulk, but all preternaturally solemn and immovable. Here and there among the faces you miss the well-known type. The thick prominent lips yield place to more delicate mouths, the shapeless nose to the slightly aquiline, for there are half-breeds here. who take more after their Indian fathers than their African mothers, and who serve as a living example of the tricks that Nature can play in the intermingling of races.

And now the piper in the corner sets up a wilder strain: the drummers work till their muscles crack, now looking as if they were undergoing torture, now turning half-round to have a joke with a fresh arrival. until the tension reaches breaking-point and with a shout some ten men dash forward and, forming a ring round the musicians, commence the wild "Bomo" dance, even as their savage ancestors were wont to do in past ages round the camp-fires of Africa. Watch them as

SIDIS OF BOMBAY.

they move round. They are obviously inspired by the noise and are bent heart and soul upon encouraging the laggards to join in. One of them, as he passes, shouts out that he sails by the P. and O. "Dindigul" the next day and intends to make a night of it; another is wearing the South African medal and says he earned it as fireman-serang on a troopship from these shores; while a third, in deference to the English guest, gives vent at intervals to a resonant "Hip, hip, Hurrah," which almost drowns the unmelodious efforts of the "maestro" with the kerosine-tin. The "Bomo" dance is followed with scarce a pause by the "Lewa," a kind of festal revel, in which the dancers move inwards and outwards as they circle round; and this in turn yields place to the "Bondogaya" and two religious figures, the "Damali" and "Chinughi," which are said when properly performed to give men the power of divination.

Long ere the "Lewa" draws to a close, the women have joined in. First two of the younger women move from the corner, one of them with eyes half-closed and preserving a curious rigidity of body even while her feet are rythmically tapping the floor: then two more join and so on, until the circumference of the dancing-circle is expanded as far as the size of the room will allow and not a single woman is left on the china matting. Some of them are as completely under the spell of the music as the men, but they exhibit little sign of pleasure or excitement on their faces; and were it not for an occasional smile or the weird shriek they raise at intervals, one might suppose them all to be in a state of hypnotism. Perchance they are. The most vivacious of them all is the old Patelni, who since the death of Queen Sophie has been in almost complete control of the female portion of the Sidi community. She has no place in the chain of dancing fanatics but stands in the centre near the drummers, now breaking into a "pas seul" on her own account, now urging a laggard with all the force of a powerful vocabulary, beating time the while upon the shoulder of the nearest drummer.

So the revel progresses, sometimes dying down into a slow movement in which only the hoarse breathing of the men, the tap-tap of female heels, is heard ; and anon breaking into a kind of gallop, punctuated with shouts of "Bravo" "Hip, hip, Hurrah" and the queer dental shriek, which our friendly serang tells us is the peculiar note of the African reveller. But at length Nature asserts her sway ; and after the dancing has lasted almost without interruption for three hours, the Sidi Patel, Hassan, gives permission for a brief recess, during which he introduces to the spectators the son of the Sidi chief Makanda,—a fine specimen of manhood whose six-foot stature belies the fact that he is still according to Sidi views a minor incapable of looking after his own interests. At this juncture too an itinerant coffee-seller limps into the room with his tin can and cups and is straightway pounced upon by the breathless performers, who apparently find coffee better dancing-powder than any other beverage.

"How much" you ask him "do you charge per cup?" "Saheb," comes the answer, "for two rupees you can treat the whole gathering, men, women and children to a cup apiece; for this coffee is of the best!" So we pay our footing in kind and bid adieu to the dancers who are prepared to continue the revels till the early hours of the morning. As we turn the corner into Ripon Road, we catch a final glimpse of our bemedalled serang executing a fandango on the doorstep, and of the Sidi Patel with a cup of hot coffee in his hand shouting in broken English, "Good-night, God Save the King!"

# XIV.

## A KONKAN LEGEND.

LEGEND and tradition have rendered many a spot in India sacrosanct for all time ; and to no tract perhaps have such traditions clung with greater tenacity than to the western littoral which in the dawn of the centuries watched the traders of the ancient world sail down from the horizon to barter in its ports. As with Gujarat and the Coast of Kathiawar, so with the Konkan it is a broken tale of strange arrivals, strange building, strange trafficking in human and inanimate freight that greets the student of ancient history and bewilders the ethnologist. The Konkan, in which in earliest days "the beasts with man divided empire claimed," and which itself is dowered with a legendary origin not wholly dissimilar in kind from the story of Rameses III and his naval conquest, offers a fair sample of these semi-historical myths in the tale of the arrival of the Chitpavans at Chiplun in Ratnagiri. For, so runs the tale, on a day long buried in the abyss of Time it chanced that a terrific storm gathered over the western waters ; and as night drew on the sky, black with serried ranks of clouds, burst into sharp jets of fire, the rain poured forth in torrents unquenchable, and the shriek of a mighty whirlwind, mingling with the deep echoes of Indra's thunder, drowned even the roar of the storm-lashed seas. Among the ships abroad on that night was one of strange device with high peaked prow. manned by a crew of fair-skinned and blue-eyed men. which was forging its way from a northern port to some fair city of Southern India; and when the storm struck her. she was not many miles from what we now call the Ratnagiri coast. Bravely did she battle with the tempest; bravely did her men essay to keep her on her course, bringing to play their hereditary knowledge of sea-craft. their innate dexterity of brain. But all their scheming, all their courage proved fruitless. As a bridegroom of old time scattering the bridal procession by the might of a powerful right arm, the sea swept away her protectors and carried her, lone and defenceless, on to the surge-beaten shore. And when morning broke Surya, rising red above the eastern hills, watched the hungry waves cast up beside her fourteen white corpses, the remnants of her crew—silent suppliants for the last great rites which open to man the passage into the next world.

Now at the ebb of the tide the dark people that dwelt upon the marge of the sea fared shorewards and found the blue-eyed mariners lying dead beside their vessel; and they. marvelling greatly what manner of men these might have been, took counsel among themselves and decided to bestow upon them the last rites of the dead. So they built a mighty funeral pyre for them with logs of resinous wood hewn in the dark forest that stretched inland, and they fortified the souls of the dead seamen with prayer and lamentation. But lo! a miracle: for as the flames hissed upwards,

Parashurama and the Chitpavans.

purging the bodies of all earthly taint, life returned to them by the grace of Parashurama; and they rose one and all from the pyre and praised Him of the Axe, in that he had raised them from the dead and made them truly "Chitta-Pavana" or the "Pyre Purified." And they dwelt henceforth in the land of the arrow of their Deliverer and were at peace, forgetting their former home and their drear wandering over the pathless sea, and taking perchance unto themselves wives from among the ancient holders of the soil. Now the place where they abode is called Chittapolana or Chiplun unto this day.

And it came to pass in the fulness of time, as the Sahyadri-khand tells, that Parashurama called all Brahmans to a great festival in the new land which he had created between the mountains and the sea. But the twice-born hearkened not to his words; whereat the God waxing wroth determined to create new Brahmans who would not turn a deaf ear to his counsel. Revolving this decision in his heart he walked down to the shore, and there in the seaward-gazing burning-ground he met a stranger-people, white-skinned, blue-eyed, and fair to look upon. and asked them who they were and whence they came. "Fishermen (or hunters) are we," they answered, "and dwell upon the sea-shore, sixty families of us in all." And the God was pleased with them and raising them to the rank of Brahmans, divided them into fourteen "Gotras," and made them a solemn promise that should they ever call him to mind in any real emergency he would come to their assistance. So they dwelt for many a day, waxing by the favour of God both numerous and learned, until by ill-hap they hearkened into evil counsel and called upon the God without just reason, And He, when he learned what they had done, was exceeding wroth and cursed them, dooming them to sorrow and to the sevice of other men so long as the sun and moon should endure. Thus the Chitpavans gained their Brahmanhood, but lost their right to superiority in that they flouted the promise of their God.

Such are the legends, popular and Puranic, of the coming of the Chitpavans to Western India. That some historic truth lies below the garbled tale of shipwreck and resurrection is partly proved by the physical traits of their descendants,—of those men, in fact, whose immediate ancestors, employed at first as messengers or spies of Maratha chieftains, by innate cleverness, tact, and faculty for management gradually welded together the loose Maratha confederacy and became directors of the internal and external politics of the Peshwa's dominions. For to this day the true Chitpavan perserves the fair skin, the strange grey eyes, the aspect of refined strength and intelligence, which must have characterized the shipwrecked mariners of old fable and marked them out in later years as strangers in a strange land. But whence came they, these foreign immigrants, who after long sojourn in the country of their adoption moved upwards to the Deccan and stood within the shadow of the Peshwa's throne? Much has been written of their origin, much that is but empty theory: but, as 'Historicus' has remarked in the columns of a local journal, the lesson to be learned from their home dialect and from their strange surnames,—Gogte, Lele, Karve, Gadre, Hingne and so on, is that the Chitpavan Brahmans of Western India came in legendary ages from Gedrosia, Kirman and the Makran coast, and that prior to their domicile in those latitudes they probably formed part of the population of ancient Egypt or Africa. That they were once a sea-faring and fishing people is proved by the large number of words of oceanic origin which still characterize their home-speech, while according to the authority above mentioned the "Chandrakant" which they recognize is not the sweating crystal of Northern India and ancient Sanskrit lore, but a fossil coral found upon the Makran coast. Forty years ago Rao Saheb V. N. Mandlik remarked that "the ancestors of the tribe probably came by ships either from some other port in India or from the opposite coast of Africa;" and in these later days his theory is corroborated by General Haig, who traces them back to the great marts on the Indus and thence still further back to the Persian Gulf and Egypt. Why or at what date they left the famous country of the Pharaohs, none can say: but that these white-skinned Brahmans are descendants of such people as the Berbers, who belonged of right to the European races, seems the most plausible theory of their origin yet put forward, and serves as an additiona proof of the enormous influence exercised upon posterity by the famous country of the Nile.

Thus perhaps the legend of storm and shipwreck is not false, but records in poetic diction the arrival on these shores of men who presumably had in some degree inherited the genius of the most famous and most civilized country of prehistoric ages, and who had by long trafficking in dangerous waters and by the hardships of long migration acquired that self-reliance and love of mastery which has been bequeathed almost unchanged to their Brahmanised descendants. The Chitpavans were indeed the children of the storm, and something of the spirit of the storm lives in them still. Some trace is theirs of the old obstinacy which taught those pale ancestors to fight against insuperable forces until they were cast naked and broken upon the sea-shore. And peradventure the secret lesson of the ancient folk-tale is this, that the God of the Axe, despite the curse, is still at hand to help them along the path to new birth, provided always that their cause is fair, that they invoke not his aid for trivial or unjust ends, and that they have been truly purified in the pyres of affliction.

## XV.

## NUR JAN.

"The singer only sang the Joy of Life,
For all too well, alas! the singer knew,
How hard the daily toil, how keen the strife,
How salt the falling tear, the joys how few."

"NAY, Saheb, I accept no money for my songs from you and your friend; for you have taken a kindly interest in me and my past history, and have shewn me the respect which my birth warrants, but which alas! my occupation hath made forfeit in the eyes of the world. But,—if you have found satisfaction in my singing, then write somewhat of me and of my Mimi to the paper, even as you did of Imtiazan, that thus your people—the people who know not the inner life of India may learn that I was not born amid the saringis and the bells, and that I, the singer, hide within my heart a life-long regret."

So she spake, seated on the clean white floor-cloth of the brightly-lighted "diwankhana," like some delicate flower cradled on a crystal lake. We had seen her once before at the house of an Indian friend, who had hospitably invited a company to witness her songs and dances; we had heard her chant the subtle melodies of Hindustan and even old English rounde-

Nur Jan.

lays for the special delectation of the English guests; we had remarked her delicate hands, the great dark eyes, the dainty profile, the little ivory feet, and above all the gentle voice and courteous bearing; and we realized that Nur Jan had not been bred to this uncurtained life, but must once have known the care, affection and the gentle training of a patrician home.

By what caprice of evil fortune had she come to this,—hiring out her voice and her nimble feet to enhance the pleasure of a chance entertainment, far from her own people and from her northern Indian home? What secret lay in the song of the frail maiden on the banks of the Jamna, in the earnest request she made to us not to mention the name of dead Royalty before her attendant-musicians? The mystery remained unsolved for that evening; and it was not till some weeks later that the chances of an official enquiry brought us face to face again. But this time the ill-starred dancing-skirt and bells had been locked away; and in their stead we saw the silken jacket, the spangled pale-blue sari, covered by a diaphanous black veil, like a thin cloud half-veiling the summer heavens, the necklace of pearls round the olive pillar of her throat, and above them the calm face and the wealth of dark hair that scorned all artificial adornment. There she sat in her own house, singing to two rich Arabs and a subordinate agent of one of the greatest rulers of Asia, while behind her Mimi, aged two years,—the legacy of a dead affection,—crooned and tried to clap her small hands in rythm with her mother's song. And in the pauses of her singing, while the musicians tightened their bows and the silver "pan-box" was passed round to her Indian-guests, she lifted a little way, a very little way the curtain of the past.

"Yea, Saheb, you have rightly spoken. I come of a good family, and as a child I was sent to school in Calcutta and learned your English tongue. When I grew to girlhood I determined to study medicine and serve the women of my faith as a doctor. But barely had I commenced the preliminary lessons of compounding when the trouble came upon our house, and my sister and I were brought away from the old home to Bombay and bidden to find the wherewithal to support those to whom we owed respect and affection. Saheb, with us the word of near relations is law, and their support a sacred duty. What could we, gently-bred Mahomedan girls, do in a strange city? We had always liked singing and had taken lessons in our home; and it seemed that herein lay the only chance of supporting ourselves and others Therefore, not without hesitation, not without tears, we bade adieu to the "pardah" of our people and cast the pearls of our singing before the public. Thus has it been since that day. My sister by good-hap has married well and regained the shelter of the curtain : but I am still unwed and must sing until the end comes."

"How can I seek help of my grandsire? Have I

not disgraced his name by adopting this life? And were I mean enough to ask his favour, would he not first insist that I become once more 'pardahnashin'? I cannot live again behind the screen, for too long have I been independent. The filly that has once run free cares not afterwards for the stall and bridle. It has been an evil mistake, Saheb, but one not of my making I sometimes loathe the lights, the tinsel, the bells, aye even the old songs; for they remind me of what I might have been, but for another's fault, and, –of what I am. You ask of Mimi's future? So long as I live, she never shall play a part in this work. Mated with a good man of mine own faith she will never know regret. That is my great wish, Saheb. The issue lies with Allah."

So the tale ran on with its accompaniment of song, its suggestion of regret. Once in the middle of a ballad a funeral passes in the street below. The mourner's chant sounds above the bourdon of the tom-tom, the wail of the saringis. "Hush, hush" cries Nur Jan, "let the dead pass in peace. It is not meet that the song of the dancing-girl should be heard upon the final journey." One more refrain, one more question on the mystery of her birth, and we ask permission to depart, offering at the same time some small token of our approval of her songs, to which she replies in the words that commence this chapter. We catch a last glimpse of her, bidding us good-bye in the gentle manner that tells its own tale, and of Mimi crooning to herself and trying to push a much-crumpled playing-card,—the Queen of Hearts,—into the cinglet of her small pyjamas.

# XVI.

# GOVERNOR AND KOLI.

## A FISHERMAN'S LEGEND.

A FRIEND has supplied me with the following quaint history of a well-known Marathi ballad, which is widely chanted by the lower classes in and around Bombay. Composed originally as a song of seed-time, it has now lost its primary significance and is sung by men at their work or by mothers hushing their children in the dark alleys of the city. The verse runs thus :—

> "Nakhwa Koli jat bholi,
> Ghara madhye dravya mahamar,
> Topiwalyane hukum kela,
> Batliwalyachya barabar."

which may be rudely interpreted as follows :—

> "Seaman Koli of simple mould
> Hath in his house great store of gold—
> Lo! at the order of Topiwala
> Koli is peer of Batliwala"!

Now the word "Topiwala" means an English-man; and "Batliwala" is a reference to the first Parsi Baronet, Sir Jamsetji Jeejeebhoy; albeit the word is often used as a synonym for "millionaire" in much the same way as "Shankershet" has crept into Marathi parlance as the equivalent of "rich and prosperous."

The story, which the Kolis relate with pride, refers to the great wealth of Zuran Patel, the ancester of Mahadev Dharma Patel who at this moment is the headman and leader of the Christian Kolis of Bombay. That Zuran Patel was a rich man can be proved from the ancient documents relating to the properties recently acquired by the Improvement Trust in and around Mandvi. For his name appears as chief owner in many of them; and it seems clear that the spoils which he gathered from the sea formed the basis of a goodly heritage upon dry land. He was an intimate friend of a certain Parsi millionaire, whom the composer of the ballad has supposed to be Sir Jamsetji Jeejeebhoy, but who was more probably a member of the great family of Wadia,—the original ship-builders and dock-masters of the East India Company.

It chanced one day that the Governor of Bombay (perhaps Lord Falkland or Lord Elphinstone) wandered into Mandvi Koliwada and came suddenly upon the Parsi and the Koli Patel sitting in converse with one another. Up rose the Parsi millionaire and made obeisance; but the Koli quite indifferent and not recognising the solitary "Topiwala," remained in his seat. His Excellency's curiosity was aroused; and asking the Parsi the name of his scantily-clad comrade, he was informed that the man was a rich fisherman, who from time to time was accustomed to spread out his

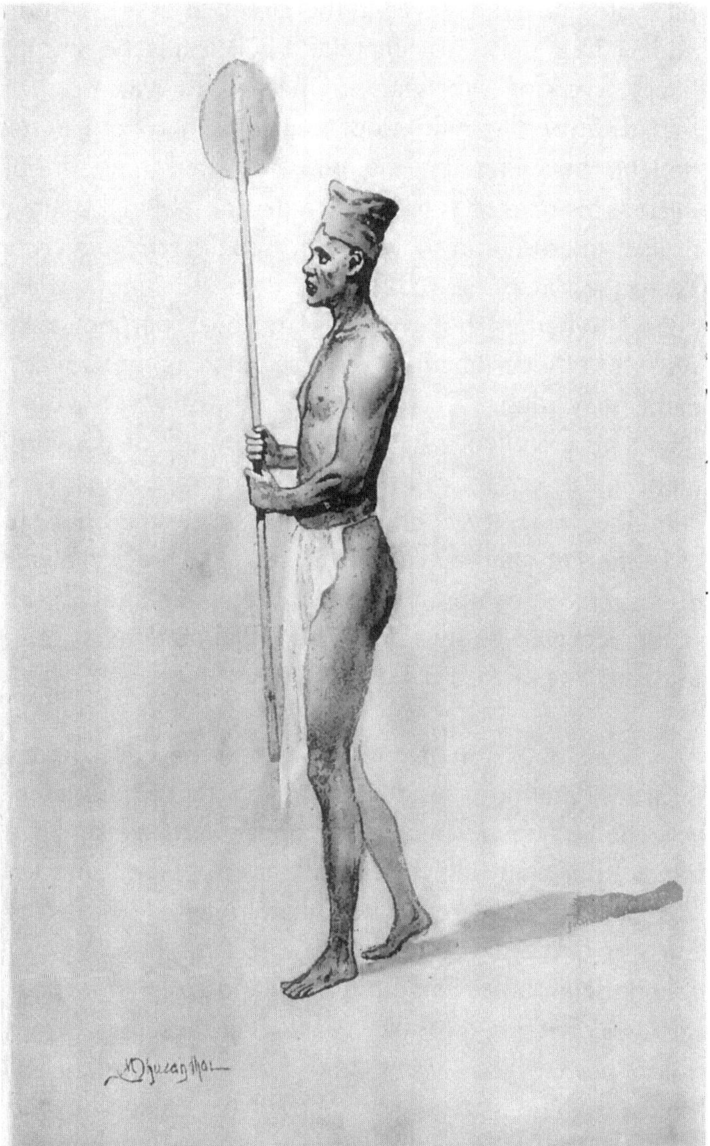

A Koli.

piles of gold and silver in the street to dry. "And" added the Parsi, "so simple and guileless is he that the people walk over the glittering heap with wax on their feet, thus robbing him in open daylight; and yet he does nought, believing that the pile of wealth must shrink even as his piles of fish shrink, when placed in the sun to dry." Interested in the man's personality, the Governor asked the Parsi to introduce the Patel to him, and enquired whether he would grant some portion of his wealth to Government. "Yes, as much as the Government may desire" was the ready answer. "But" quoth his Excellency, "what will you ask of Government in return?" "Only this," answered the Koli. that Government will grant me the exclusive privilege of roofing my house with silver tiles." After some little discussion, a compromise was effected: and Zuran Patel received permission, as a special mark of favour, to place a few copper tiles above his house.

The house in Dongri Street, where Mahadev Dharma Patel now resides, is reputed to be the identical house upon which the copper tiles were once fixed. But many alterations have taken place, and the tiles have disappeared. For many years, so runs the tale, they were preserved as a sort of family escutcheon, being taken off the roof and fixed in a conspicuous position in the wall. Perhaps they were stolen, perhaps they were worn away by constant polishing, Who can say? They have passed beyond the realm of fact to that of legend. Suffice it to say that the Kolis firmly believe the whole story, and add that Zuran Patel's house was the only real strong-house in Bombay at that epoch, the walls being built upon a framework of iron girders and the cellar, containing the piles of silver, being stouter than a modern safe. It seems not improbable that the old cellars of Mandvi Kolivada were originally the colouring-ponds of the fishermen, which, as building progressed and crowding set in, were enclosed with tiles and brick and mortar and utilised as store-rooms.

Such is the history of the quaint ballad of the English Governor, the Parsi millionaire, and the Koli Patel. It seems to us to crystallise the honourable connection and friendship which has existed from the earliest days of British rule in Bombay between the aboriginal-fishermn, the Parsi pioneers of commerce and the English Government in the person of its highest representative. It recalls to us the days of siege and warfare when the Governor of the struggling settlement sought the help of the sturdy fishermen and when Rustom Dorabji put himself at their head, formed them into a rudely-drilled corps, and drove the Sidi off the island. It recalls the action of the Honourable Thomas Hodges in their behalf a century and a half ago, and the subsequent confirmation of their ancient rights by Sir James Fergusson and Sir Bartle Frere. And lastly it represents a belief, which has attained almost the sanctity of religion in the heart of Kolidom, that between themselves and the King's representative in Bombay there exists a bond of good-feeling and respect which dating as it does from 1675 has been welded firm by time and shall never be broken.

## XVII.

## THE TRIBE ERRANT.

IN the more thickly-populated quarters of the city of Bombay—quarters that are rarely explored by the European, a succession of criers and hawkers pass through the streets from morn till eve and sometimes far into the night. In the early morning, before the house-sparrow has chirped himself and his family into wakefulness, you catch the doleful and long-drawn cry of the early Fakir or Mahomedan beggar, whose object is not so much to wake the Faithful and bid them remember "the prayer that is better than sleep" as to be the earliest bird to catch the mouthful of Moslem charity. Watch him as he awakens the echoes of the quarter by repeating in the most melancholy tones Ali's famous gift of his sons to the beggars of the Hegira or some other great tradition of the generosity of Ali, set to verse for the special behoof of his brotherhood by some needy poetaster like the famous Nazir of Agra. He is followed by another who chants in deep bass tones a legend explanatory of the virtues of the great saint of Baghdad. But Ali is the favourite of the beggar-tribe, because forsooth the beggar runs no risk in singing his praises. If one glorify the other three Khalifas in a Sunni quarter, it is well with one, but not so in an area devoted to the Shia population: and so the beggar

A Deccani Fruit-seller.

chooses Ali's name as a convenient and fitting means of opening the purse-strings of both the great Musulman sects.

As the day dawns, sturdy Hyderabad chorus-singers pass along the streets chanting the "prayers for the Prophet" in voices that awaken the denizens of the dark garrets and hidden courts of the teeming chals. And after them come the beggars of that class which is the peculiar product of Mahomedan life in Bombay. As the majority of the middle-class Musulmans and all the poorer class live in chals or "malas,"—each family occupying one or at most two rooms in a building, the passages, corridors and staircases of these human warrens become the chosen paths of those astute mendicants who disdain not, when chance offers, to turn their hand to a little quiet thieving. Even as they fare upon their rounds, you catch the welcome call of the vendor of "jaleibi malpurwa," who sells wheat-cakes fried rarely in *ghi* and generally in oil, and the "jaleibi" a sort of macaroni fried likewise in oil. These crisp cakes are a favourite breakfast-dish of the early-rising factory-operative, who finds himself thus saved the drudgery of cooking when he is barely awake and when moreover he is in a hurry to reach the scene of his daily labours. The vendor of these dainties is truly "a study in oils," and his hands, which serve the purpose of knife and fork for the separation of his customers' demands, drip but not with myrrh. Though a vendor of oleaginous dainties, he is himself far from well-nourished. You can see his collar-bone and count his ribs and almost mark the beatings of his poor profit-counting heart. A dirty dhoti girds his loins, and upon his head is a turban of the same questionable hue which serves both as a head-dress and as a support for his tray of cakes. If a Musulman, he wears only a skullcap, a shirt or jacket and a pair of soiled baggy trousers. Once he has called, the jaleibi-vendor has a habit of presenting himself every day at the very hour when the children of the house begin to clamour for food, and calmly defies the angry order of the householder not to appear unless bidden.

Next comes the vendor of "chah, chah garam, chaaah garaaam" or hot tea, who is unusually an Irani. For having introduced tea into Western Asia the inhabitants of the land of "the gul and the bulbul" claim the secret of making a perfect infusion of the celestial leaves. He is no longer the embodiment of Tom Moore's Heroic Guebre, this tea-vending Irani, and his apron forbids the suggestion that he has any association with Gao, the subverter of a monarchy and the slayer of the tyrant Zuhhac. He has sadly degenerated from the type of his Guebre ancestor. If he owns a shop he combines the sale of other commodities with the tea business. He has an ice-cream, a sherbet and a "cold-drink" department; and he touts for customers, singing the praises of hot and cold beverages in a language redolent of Persian. It does not pay him to use fresh tea-leaves from Kangra or China; so he purchases his stock from small traders, who in their turn obtain it as a bargain from butlers or stewards. The latter dry them after one infusion by their masters and, mixing some unused leaves, make up a fresh box and dispose of it in the markets. As for soda-water and allied beverages, he gets his supply from the cheapest manufacturers; while his ice-cream contains probably more water than milk and is flavoured, not with vanilla, pine-apple or orange, but with some article which he declares is a complete antidote against internal discomfort. He prepares his tea *a la Russe* in a brightly-polished samovar which compares favourably with his tea-cups and country-made tin spoons. He charges his customer from two to four pice for this delightful mixture which has a flavour of hot-water and iron-rust rather than of tea.

Here too comes the itinerant fruit-seller, very often a woman, who hawks fruit of all kinds from the superior mango to the acid "karaunda" of the Ghats. For the sale of country-mangoes a place of vantage is required; so she takes up a strong position on the road-side or on the doorstep of a house and sets to work to pick out her best fruit and place it on the top of her basket. She is generally a Deccani, either Musulman or Hindu, varying in age from 20 to 40 and is fully capable of conciliating the Lord of the Bombay pavements, when he somewhat roughly commands her to move on. "Jemadar Saheb" she calls him; and if this flattery is insufficient she offers one of her ripest mangoes with a glance that he cannot resist. It is too much for the sepoy: he smiles and tramps off, and she holds her position undisturbed. If she be a Hindu, you

The Coffee-seller.

will probably notice the bright-red mark on her forehead, joining brow to brow, or, in the words of a Persian poet, uniting two Parthian or Tartar bows into Kama's Long-bow. The male mango-hawker is a Deccan Hindu or Musulman gardener who purchases a stock of showy inferior fruit from the wholesale dealers. After the mango season is over he becomes a vendor of Poona figs or Nagpur oranges. He is often a small, dark, muscular man who began life as a day-labourer in the highly-cultivated fields of the Deccan and has journeyed to the city with his modest savings tightly tied up in his waist-cloth in the hope of eventually cutting as big a figure in the village home as does his friend Arjuna, who some years ago returned to his village as a capitalist and is even now the bosom-friend of the Patel.

The itinerant coffee-vendor is a characteristic feature of the Musulman quarters of Bombay. Of Arab or Egyptian origin, this coffee-trade immediately proved attractive to the Musulman public and, inasmuch as it requires little stock or capital, has been a boon to many a poor Mahomedan anxious to turn an honest penny. The "kahwe-wala" has no cry and yet manages to proclaim his presence by sounds which are audible in the inmost darkness of the chals. He is the beetle of the pedlar tribe. He does not sing, he does not cry—he stridulates. Carrying in his hand a large number of small coffee-cups, fitted one within another, he strikes them together like a string of castanets, while in the left hand he bears a portable stove-like article on which rests his tin or copper kettle.

His entire stock-in-trade, including the ground coffee in his kettle, does not as a rule exceed five rupees in value. The "kahwe-wala" belongs to three nationalities, Arab, Negro and Native Indian. If an Arab, he may be a disabled sailor or the retired body-servant of some Arab merchant; if an Indian, he is usually an old resident of the city, experienced in the wiles of the urban population and sometimes perhaps a protégé of the local police. He has a perfect acquaintance with the intricacies of Bombay galis and back-slums; he is a creature of jovial temper, being hail-fellow-well-met with most of his customers, and he is not a grasping creditor. His account, which he notes down on whitewashed walls, sometimes reaches the sum of Rs. 10 to Rs. 15 where thriftless wives are concerned. Generally the score is paid: but if it be shirked or disputed, he never thinks of invoking legal aid for the recovery of his money. He has an abiding faith in the doctrine of "Live and let live."

## XVIII.

# THE PANDU-LENA CAVES.

### A NASIK PILGRIMAGE.

NASIK! What a story the name evokes! Nasik the Lotus-city, Nasik the home of Gods; who has borrowed her name from the nine hills which lay within the compass of her sacred walls. For we like not, nor do we believe, that alternative derivation of the name from "Nasika," a nose, in allusion to the fate which here overtook the demon Shurpanakhi. It is altogether too savage an appellation for a city whose purity was established in the "Krita Yuga," and whose fame is coeval with that of the great protagonists of Hindu myth and epic. The great city of religion in the West stood upon seven hills, the holy city of the East stood upon nine; and the famous rivers which flow past them whisper in each case of a heritage of undying renown. Fancy hand in hand perhaps with a substratum of historical truth has discovered traces of Rama's chequered life, of Sita's devotion in many spot within the limits of Nasik. The Forest of Austerity (Tapovan), Panchvati and Ramsej or Ram's seat, that strangely-shaped hill fortress to the north of Nasik, are but three of the holy places which appeal so forcibly to the hearts of the people as the visible legacies of divine life on earth.

But to us the temples and the sacred pools seem nothing by comparison with the mighty monuments of Buddhism, which local wiseacres have erroneously named the Pandu-Lena or caves of the Pandavas. We drive out in the fresh morning air along the trunk road, which extends southwards of the holy city like a grey ribbon streaked by two parallel lines of lighter colour where the wheels of the bullock-carts have ground the hard metal into dust; and hard by the fifth milestone we come face to face with three stark hills, standing solitary out of the plain. A congeries of Mhars' huts fringing the roadside marks the most convenient spot for alighting, whence we strike across the belt of level land which divides the highway from the foot of the easternmost of the triad of hills. "Trirashmi" or Triple Sunbeam is the name by which the hill is known in seven of the cave-inscriptions, and is held by the learned Pundit who wrote the *Gazetter* account to refer to its pyramidal or triple fire-tongue shape. But is it not conceivable that the hand which carved the earliest of those priceless inscriptions desired to designate the triad of contiguous hills as "the tripla ray," and not the eastern hill alone in which the caves have been hewn? Who can tell? When we recall the almost unbroken chain of caves,—the Shivner, the Ganesh, the Manmoda and the Tulja,—which surround Junner, we suspect that the original intention of those primeval devotees was to carve dwellings and chapels in all three hills, which thus would have surely formed a triple beam of light in honour of the great Master, whom an English missionary has characterized as "one of the grandest examples of self-denial and love to humanity which the world has ever produced." A narrow and devious path, worn by the feet of worshipers, leads upward to the broad terrace which fronts the caves. Here you are sheltered from the wind, and peace inviolate broods upon these dwellings of a vanished people ; but turn your steps round the western corner and the boisterous breeze will quickly chase you back behind the sheltering bulwarks of the hill.

Of the twenty-four caves all except the eighteenth or chapel-cave were originally *layanas* or monastic dwellings and contained no images when first their makers gazed upon their work and found it good. But long after their earliest inmates had conquered Desire and had gained Nirvana for their souls the followers of the Mahayana school from Northern India took the dwellings for their own use and carved out of the austere walls of their precursors' cells those images and idols which are now the chief feature of the caves. Buddha seated upon the lion-throne and the figures of his Bodhisattvas with their fly-whisks are symbols of a later and more idolatrous form of Buddhism and are several centuries later than the days (b. c. 110) when the great monk (Sramana) fashioned the nineteenth cave in the reign of Krishna the Satakarni. Nor has Vandalism in the guise of the Mahayana school been alone at work here. The tenth cave once contained a relic-shrine or *dagoba* similar to the relic-shrines at Karli, Shivner and Ganesh Lena; but in its place now stands a hideous figure of Bhairav aflame with red-lead, and nought remains to testify to the former presence of the shrine save the Buddhist T capital, the umbrellas and the flags which surmounted it. The eleventh cave bears traces of Jain sacrilege in the blue figure of the Tirthankar or hierach who sits cross-legged in the back wall and in the figure of Ambika on the right. But the most conspicuous example of the alteration of ancient monuments to suit the needs of late comers is the twentieth cave, where the colossal Buddha, who muses with his attendants in the dense darkness of the inner shrine, has been smeared with black pigment and adorned with gold tinsel and is proudly introduced to you by the local *pujari* as Dharmaraja, the eldest of the five Pandavas, the surrounding Bodhisattvas being metamorphosed into Nakula, Sahadeva, Bhima, Arjuna, Krishna and Draupadi, the joint wife of the five! Alas for "the Perfect One" in whose honour, as the inscription tells us, "the wife of the great war-lord Bhavagopa" commenced building the cave in B. C. 50. He has long been forgotten and the hand which he uplifts in token of the Four Verities, discovered after great agony and temptation beneath the Tree of Wisdom, is now pointed out as the wrathful hand of the demi-god of the Mahabharata. Once and once only in these later days has the Buddha evinced his displeasure at the modernization of his ancient shrine. About the year 1880 came hither a Bairagi, naked and wild, who walled off a corner of the cave and raised a clay altar to his puny god. Sacrilege intolerable! And the Buddha through the hand of an avaricious Koli smote him unto death and hurled his naked corpse down hill. The titanic figure is still worshipped by the Hindus: flowers and lighted lamps are daily offered up to him by the ignorant Hindu priest; but he sits immutable, inarticulate, content in the knowledge that to them that have understanding his real message of humanitarianism speaks through the clouds of falsehood which now enwrap his Presence.

Much might be written of the strange medley of creeds which are symbolised in these caves. The Nagdevas with their serpent-canopies, which are relics of a primordial Sun and Serpent worship totally foreign to pure Buddhism, appear side by side with the Swastika or Life-symbol of the greater creed, with the lotus and other symbols of a phallic cult, and as in the small cistern near cave 14 with the female face representing the low-class Hindu belief in the divinity of the small-pox. Jain images of a later school of Buddhism, dating from the 5th or 6th century after Christ, have helped to rob these homes of Buddhist mendicants of their original simplicity and severity, and have rendered it almost impossible for any save the wise men of the East to read their chequered history aright. In almost the last cave we entered, where two standing figures on the right and left mount guard over the well-known image of the Master, our footsteps roused a large female rat and her young, which crawled up the silent seated figure and took refuge on the very crown of its head. Sanctuary! So we turned aside to scrutinise the strange symbolical figures of the twenty-fourth cave and the stories of the chaste and unchaste wives which are hewn in the ornamental gateway of the third.

From the terrace in front of the caves a fine panorama greets the eye. Below commences the wide plain which creeps northwards to the rugged hills comprising the weird couch-shaped summit of Ramsej and the solitary cone of the Chambhar Hill, embosoming the great Jain caves of the 12th century. Beyond the Chambhar cone climb heavenwards the castellated pinnacles of the Chandor range, mist-shrouded in this monsoon season. In the nearer distance the primeval Brahman settlement of Govardhan sleeps amid her mango-groves, and opposite to it the modern Christian village of Sharanpur marks the threshold of that tract of fair woodland and fairer garden which is Nasik's pride. Here and there a red roof catches the sun's rays and shows a splash of orange amid the green; but save for this the picture has but two tints, the warm green of the plain country in the foreground and the grey of the mighty mountain-range which stands sentinel behind it. Your feet rest upon soil hallowed by the memories of two thousand years, upon ground which bears the sign-manual of early and late Buddhist, of Jain and lastly of Maratha, who used the hill as a muster-ground of warriors and bored holes in the graven images for the tethering of his cattle and steeds. By some divine decree "the imperial banditti" kept their impious hands from the famous inscriptions which are the real glory of these caves and form the connecting-link between ourselves and that great king whose face was "as the sun-kissed lotus, whose army drank the waters of three oceans," Shri Gautamiputra the Satakarni.

And so ends our morning's exploration. One last visit to the silent keepers of these messages from dead monarchs—and we pass down to the high road, whence we look back once more upon Trirashmi, the casket of jewels without price, and her twin sisters gleaming in the morning light like the triple prongs of some giant Trident set there by Nature in honour of the great apostle of Humanity.

## XIX.

## FATEH MUHAMMAD.

WE had wandered off the main thoroughfare, where the trams, hurtling past the Irani's tea shop, drown from time to time the chatter of Khoda Behram's clientele; and skirting a group of Mahomedans who nightly sit in solemn conclave, some on the 'otlas,' others on charpoys or chairs placed well in the fairway of traffic, we reached at length a sombre and narrow 'gali,' seemingly untenanted save by the shadows. Here a sheeted form lay prone on the roadside; there a flickering lamp disclosed through the half-open door a mother crooning to her child, while her master smoked the hubble-bubble with the clay bowl and ruminated over the events of the day,—the villainy of the landlord who contemplated the raising of the rent and the still greater rascality of the landlord's 'bhaya' who insisted upon his own 'dasturi' as well. Here a famished cat crouched over a pile of garbage hard by the sweeper's 'gali': there on the opposite side of the road a Marwadi with the features of Mephistopheles dozed over his account book; and a little further away a naked child was dipping her toes in a pool of sullage water that had dripped from the broken pipe athwart the house wall. Darkness reigned on the upper floors. At intervals a faint glimmer might be discerned behind the sodden 'chicks' which shrouded the windows; and once the stillness was broken by a voice humming a refrain from an Indian drama:—

"Jahan jahan mukam rahe, amne jhulakiram rahe,
Safarse ghar ko to phire, Aman-chaman khuda rakhe."

Which, being interpreted, runs:—"Wheresoever thou mayst halt, may God protect thee! When thou hast returned, may God give thee His peace!" The singer was invisible, but around the words of her song one could conjure up pictures of the sturdy serang asleep in the foc'sle of some westward-flying steamer, or haply of the bearded trader afare through the passes of the North-West Frontier, the while his wife in the small upper room waited with prayers for his home-coming, even as the lady of Ithaca waited for the man of many wiles.

At length we reached a small doorway which opened into a cavern black as Erebus. For a moment we paused undecided; and then out of the darkness crawled an aged Mahomedan bearing a tiny cocoanut-oil lamp. Lifting it above his head he pointed silently to a rickety staircase in the far corner, up which we groped our way with the help of a rope pendent from an upper beam. Up and up we mounted, now round a sharp corner, now down a narrow passage: the stairs swayed and shook; the air was heavy with a mixture of frankincense and

Fateh Muhammad

sullage; until at last we crawled through a trap-door that opened as by magic, and found ourselves at our journey's end.

Imagine a small attic, some fifteen feet by ten, under the very eaves of the 'chal,' filled with the smoke of frankincense so pungent that the eyes at once commenced to water nor ceased until we were once again in the open air. In one corner was spread a coarse sheet with a couple of pillows against the wall, upon which the silent Mahomedan bade us by a sign recline: in the opposite corner a 'panja,'—a species of altar smothered in jasmine wreaths and surmounted by a bunch of peacock's feathers; and immediately in front of this an earthen brazier of live charcoal. Behind the brazier sat three persons,– Fateh Muhammad, a Musalman youth with curiously large and dreamy eyes, and two old Musalman beldames, either of whom might have sat as a model for the witch of Endor. The three sat unmoved, blinking into the live charcoal, save at rare intervals when the elder of the two women cast a handful of fragrance upon the brazier and wrapped us all in a fresh pall of smoke which billowed round the room and lapped the interstices of the rotten tiles. Only the peacock's eyes in the corner never lost their lustre, staring wickedly through the smoke-wreaths like the head of Argus.

Then on a sudden the youth shivered, fell forward with his face over the brazier, and rose again to a sitting posture with eyes closed and every muscle in his body taut as though stricken by a sudden paralysis. "The spirit has entered," whispered my friend, and even as he spoke I saw the youth's throat working as if an unseen hand were kneading the muscles, and forth from his lips echoed the words "La illaha illallah illahi laho." He was deep in a trance, the curtains of his eyes half-dropped, looking as one that is dead; and the voice with which he spoke was not the voice of Fateh Muhammad, "La illaha illallah illahi laho" ! and as the words died away one that was present passed two green limes into his left hand and asked for a sign. "I am fain to journey to Lahore, starting on Tuesday next. Will it be well," he said; and after a pause came the answer "Set not forth on Tuesday, for the stars be against thy journeying; but send thine agent on Thursday and go thyself, if need be, two days later." As the message died away, the trap-door in the floor was slowly tilted upwards and through the opening crawled an obvious member of the Dhobi class. He slid forward almost to the feet of the dreaming youth and, placing as before two green limes in his hand, spoke saying "Master, my wife hath written from our country, bidding me to go unto her nor tarry by the road. But there is work toward here and the purse is light. Is it that I should go?" "La illaha illallah illahi laho!" "Aye, go unto her, lest evil haply befall thee; for much is there that is hid from thine eyes,"

Thus the seance went forward. For twenty minutes or more odd waifs and strays of humanity crawled in through the trap-door, obtained their message of good or ill, and departed into the shadows as silently as they had come. Among them were several women, one of whom sought a cure for her sick child, whimpering over the symptoms of his malady. "Meningitis, I expect," muttered my friend the doctor; but the answer came swift and sure "Bind thou the 'tawiz' round his brows and carry him to the shrine of Miran Datar, whence cometh thy help." "La illaha illallah illahi laho!"

The end came suddenly. After the last visitor had vanished through the floor there was dead silence for three minutes, while Fateh Muhammad wrestled with the spirit within him; and then with chest heaving and hands convulsively grasping the heavy air, he fell prone upon his face and lay still. The two old women moved forward and commenced making passes over his body, murmuring the while some charm, and as they waved the seven-knotted handkerchief above his head he regained consciousness and sat slowly up, "breathing like one that hath an evil dream" and bearing upon his features the signs of deathly fatigue. By this time the attic was almost clear of smoke; the guttering wick of the only oil-lamp was nearly burnt through, and Fateh Muhammad was fain to sleep. Wherefore we thanked him for permitting us this glance behind the curtain of his daily life, then crawled through the trap, slid down the reeking staircase and gained the street. One last glance, as my eyes reached the floor-level of the trap, showed me that the room was untenanted, save by the prostrate form of the visionary, above whom the eyes of the peacock still glinted with something of mockery in their blue depths

As we passed homewards down the street we heard the woman in the upper chamber still singing her prayer, but with a note of hope in its cadence :—

> "O dilruba tu gam na kho, khuda hamen baham kare"
> "Janejahan bhulo nahi, karim sada karam kare."
> "Grieve not, heart of my heart, for God will order our meeting! Soul of the world, forget not ; and may the peace of God be on us twain."

Perchance she also, like Fateh Muhammad's guests, had caught a message of good hap from out the darkness.

And so back to the light and the noise of the City's greatest artery.

# XX.

## THE TILAK RIOTS.

### A. REMINISCENCE.

*(Written August. 1908)*

AFFAIRS in the City may now be regarded as having resumed their normal course, and the chance of further disorder seems for the present to have been obviated. One of the most curious features of the disturbances was the difference of feeling exhibited by the two classes of mill-operatives, namely the Ghatis and the Malwanis. Of the whole mill-population one would have assumed that the Kunbis from the Deccan, where Tilak is stated to have so great a following, would have shown a greater disposition to riot in consequence of his arrest and conviction than the men from Ratnagiri. And yet so far as I could judge the Ghatis were far less interested in the trial and were much less disposed to express their resentment than the latter class, which comprises one or two extremely hot-headed and uncompromising individuals. The Ghatis of Sewri ndeed fat the very height of the riots, informed an Englishman with whom they are familiar, that they wonld sooner die for him than do him any harm, and their words carried home the conviction that they felt no personal sorrow at Tilak's well-deserved fate and that they would be ready in an emergency, as they have often been in past history, to stand staunchly by the side of any individual whom they know and who has been kind to them. The attitude of the Ratnagiri hands must in my opinion have been engendered by continuous and careful tuition; and this was particularly the case in the Currey Road and Delisle Road areas where agents, belonging to their own native district, had been suborned by the seditionary party to stir up trouble.

No less remarkable was the quaint juxta-position during the height of the riots of seething disorder and the quiet prosecution of their daily avocations by the bulk of the people. An officer of one of the regiments quartered on the City during the trial in the High Court gave expression to this fact in the following words :—"Warfare I understand; but this sort of business beats me altogether. At the top of the street there is a native "tamasha" with people singing and beating tom-toms; half-way down the street there are stone-throwing and firing, and at the bottom of the street there are people, Europeans and Natives, shopping! He was struck, as I was, by the incongruity of the whole business. At Jacob's Circle there was a great display of military and magisterial strength. Tommy Atkins had taken up a strong position at the corner of Clerk Road; sentries paced up and down by day and night; machine guns gaped upon the fountain erected to the memory of Le Grand Jacob. At intervals a squadron of cavalry dashed into the open, halted for a space, and then as suddenly disappeared; and they were followed by motor cars and carriages containing Commissioners, Deputy Commissioners, Police Subordinates, Special Magistrates and miscellaneous European sight-seers. All the pomp and circumstance of Law and Order were represented there, and there could scarcely have been a greater display of armed force, more secret consultations, more wild dashes hither and thither, more troubled parleying, if the entire City north of Jacob's Circle had been in flames. And yet behind it and around it the daily life of the people moved forward in its accustomed channel, The Bhandari's liquor-shop at the corner had its full complement of patrons, and the Bhandari himself might be seen pulling out handfuls of thirst-producing parched gram for those of his customers who desired a relish with their liquor; memebrs of that degraded class which follows one of the immemorial vices of the East wandered round the Marwaris' shops, begging and clapping their hands in the manner peculiar to them; and across the diameter of the Circle strayed a group of Barots—those strange semi-gipsy looking men from Kathiawar who act as priests and magicians to the Bhangi population. Seeing the military and police they halted for a moment and gave one time to have. a word with them:—"Whither go ye?" we asked, and they replied that they were bound to the big Bhangi settlement that lies not far from the Circle.

One of them carried a " bina," a second an ordinary school-slate covered with crude cabalistic signs and a third a rude book, something like a Vani's "chopda," filled with Marathi characters, which doubtless plays a part in the fortune-telling and spirit-scaring that form the stock-in-trade of these wandering hierophants. Hardly had they disappeared than four Sadhus hove in sight. One of them, who was smeared with ashes from head to foot, the lobes of whose ears had been pierced and dragged down till they nearly touched his shoulders, and who wore an enormous rosary of Rudraksha berries, acted as the spokesman of the party and stated that they were on their way to Nasik. They had come from Benares, he said, and had spent a week in the shady compound of the Mahalaksmi temple, where all the Bairagis, Gosavis and Fakirs of the Indian continent from time to time congregate. "Do you walk to Nasik or go by rail" we asked. "By rail" replied the silver-man. "But surely the true Sadhu shou!d walk, taking no heed of horse-vehicle or fire-carriage," whereat the little fat ascetic with the gourd smiled pleasantly and made some remark to the effect that all methods of conveyance are permitted to the truly devout.

So they passed down Ripon Road towards the heart of the City. Followed a couple of Muhammadan Kasais driving a small flock of sheep, dyed pink and blue in patches, which they urged forward in approved Native fashion by driving the fingers into the base of the hindmost animal's spine; and after them wandered a Syed in a faded green silk robe and cap, carrying the inevitable peacock feather brush, which plays so large a part in exorcism and divination. Later in the day a Hindu lady-doctor hurried past on her way home, and four youths of the student-class, who had left their legal studies in the Fort to see what was toward in the northern portion of the Island. A Municipal sweeper lurched across the open and proceeded to spend twenty minutes in brushing the grating of a drain, leaving the accumulated filth of the adjoining gutter to fester and pollute the surroundings; and two elderly cooly-women, each carrying a phenomenal head-load of dung-cakes, becoming suddenly aware of the presence of troops and thereby struck with terror, collided violently with one another and shot the entire contents of their baskets on to the road. This caused some amusement to the passers-by, particularly to a Pathan who had just taken a very complete bath under one of the taps of the memorial fountain, but the trouble was soon mended by a small boy who, bribed by the offer of one dung cake, helped the old ladies to re-pack their burders and replace them on their heads. Next came a swarthy gentleman from Palanpur, who said he was a hawker of glass sugar-bowls, and produced one bowl without a top as proof of his profession. He struck me as being uncommonly and perhaps designedly vacant in speech and appearance, and seemed to have no stock of glassware whatever. I am still wondering whether that topless bowl was really his own or whether he may not have filched it from some convenient dispense-khana.

Meanwhile the Irani at the corner where the trams halt did a roaring trade. He must have boiled his tea-leaves four and five times over in order to supply the constant demands for "adha kop chha-a," preferred by casual visitors who had come up out of the City to see what was going on. Memons, Bohras, Khojas, Jews, Eurasians and Europeans all patronized his shop during the days of tumult, and the amount of soda-water, "pick-me-up" and raspberryade which was consumed was phenomenal. It was as good as a play to watch the constant stream of people who came out to have a look at the soldiers and to hear their remarks on the situation. "I have heard," one of them would begin,—and then followed a string of the wildest bazaar-rumours, interspersed with many a "tobah" (fie) "iman-se" (honestly or truly) or "mag kai" (what happened next), which apparently produced such a hunger and thirst that the Irani, thanking his stars for the outbreak of disorder, had to ransack all his cases for comestibles, aerated waters and tea. They sat in deep attention when Motor Car No. O swung out of De Lisle Road and halted near the fountain; they watched with animation the Punjab cavalry trot homewards to their lines after a scurry in Kalachauki; and they burst into merriment when a refractory mule deposited one of the Northampton Regiment plump in the muddiest portion of the Circle. They had a thoroughly interesting week, these sight-seers; but not half so interesting as he did, who watched them and chatted with them and spent hours interrogating the human flotsam and jetsam of this City of a myriad castes.